SCREW MOTIVATION

WHY YOU DON'T NEED TO FEEL LIKE IT TO DO IT

OMIR DZELILOVIC

CONTENTS

PART THREE
HOW TO NOT QUIT

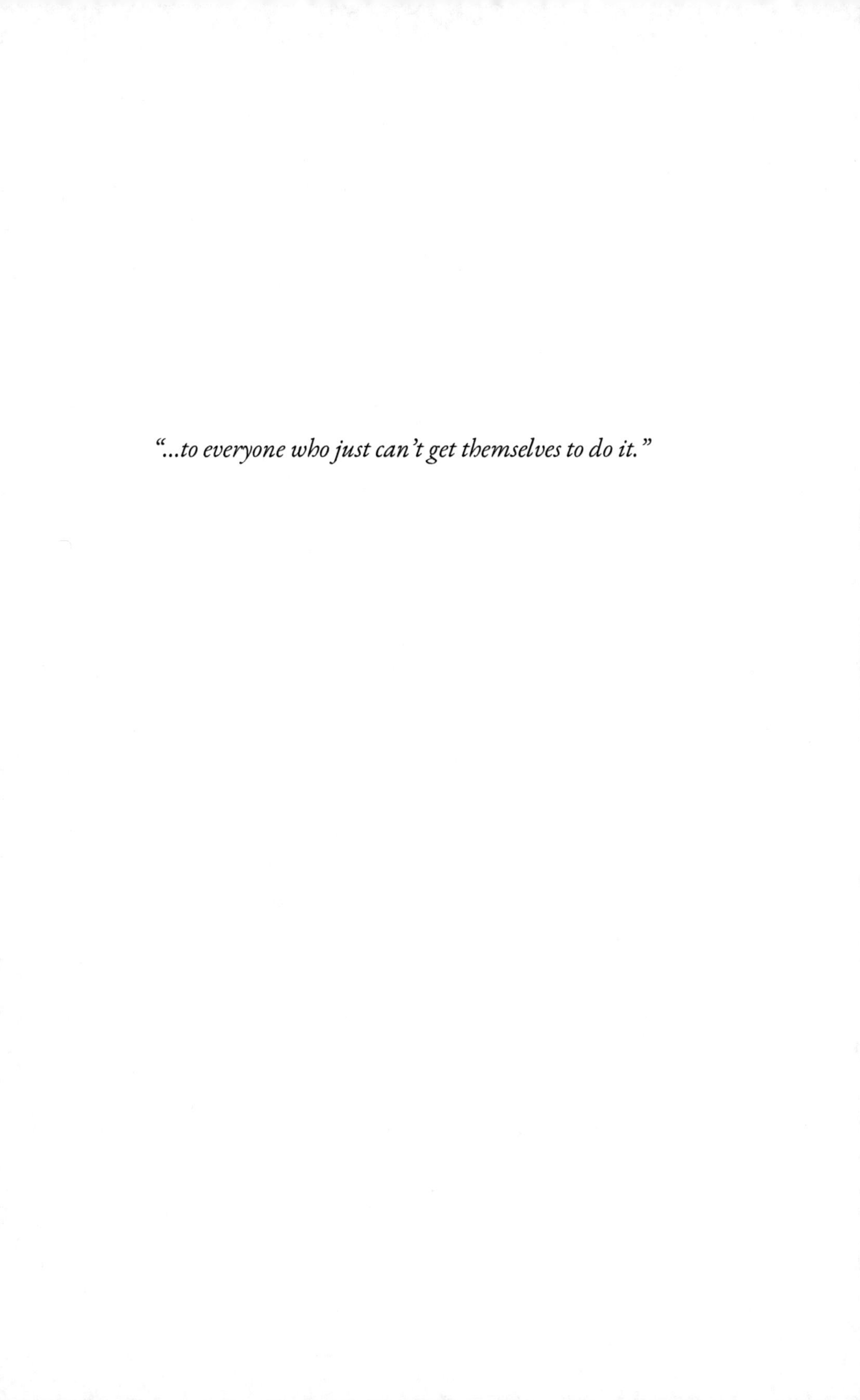

"...to everyone who just can't get themselves to do it."

WHY THIS BOOK?

If you've ever said you'd do something, planned for it, really meant it —but when the time came, you just couldn't make yourself "do it" because you didn't feel like it—this book is for you.

Maybe you wanted to start exercising, study regularly, build your business, or finally tackle that work project. You knew it was important, but when it was time to act, you just couldn't make yourself *do it.*

This book is here to change that.

A few years ago, I reached a crossroads. I was at a breaking point. My business was struggling. I was overweight. My finances were a mess. My relationships were strained. No matter how much I tried to change, I couldn't make it stick. I felt stuck—hopeless and helpless, trapped in a loop of starting and stopping, taking one step forward and two steps back.

Then one day, I realized I couldn't keep playing this game with myself. If I wanted things to change, I had to stop making excuses, stop waiting for motivation, and start doing what I knew I needed to do.

That was my turning point.

This book is the result of my journey out of that low point. I learned what it really takes to break free from feeling stuck and actually start moving forward.

Today, my life looks completely different. I recently completed my first half-marathon. I run 10k every night. My business is growing, and my relationships have never been better. I achieved this by mastering one critical skill: the ability to *do it*—even when I didn't feel like it.

I truly believe that developing the skill of *doing it*—no matter how you feel—is one of the most valuable skills you can ever learn. It's the foundation for everything else you want to accomplish. Once you know you can count on yourself to "do it" no matter how you feel, no goal feels impossible.

The ideas in this book will show you how to do just that.

When you finish this book, my promise is simple: You'll know how to make yourself do the things you want to do—even when, and especially when, you don't feel like it. Procrastination, hesitation, and the constant struggle to "make yourself do it" will be things of the past.

You'll learn that you don't actually need motivation to take action. It's not about motivation—it's about something deeper. This book will show you exactly what that is and how to tap into it.

• **Why motivation is a myth** and why you don't need it to take action.

• **The 6 hidden forces** that keep you stuck and how to unlock them (hint: it's not about willpower).

• **Practical mental techniques to overcome resistance**—even when it's at its strongest.

• **How to keep going without quitting**—the mindset behind lasting, sustainable change.

And much, much more.

So if you're ready to stop overthinking, procrastinating, and telling yourself "I'll do it tomorrow," and start becoming the person who *does*, then let's begin.

HOW TO USE THIS BOOK

This book is divided into **three parts**. Each part builds on the last, helping you understand the full picture of why you can't get yourself to do it, how to get yourself to do it and how to keep doing it for a long time.

In Part One, we'll set the groundwork. Here, you'll learn why motivation is a misnomer and why you don't actually need it to get yourself to take action. You'll learn the hidden forces of resistance that are holding you back from "doing it" and how they often mask themselves as procrastination or lack of willpower.

In Part Two, you'll learn specific techniques and strategies to overcome resistance. This section is all about actionable steps you can apply immediately to get yourself to follow through.

In Part Three, you'll learn how to make these new behaviors stick. You'll uncover the key mindsets behind lasting change, and learn how to "not quit"—after just a week or two, but to stay at it for as long as it takes to create lasting habits.

You can use this book in whichever sequence you want. If you want to dive into practical tools and techniques that you can apply today, go ahead and jump to Part Two. But if you'd like to understand the full picture—why you struggle with getting yourself to do it, how to shift your mindset, and ultimately how to become the person who "just does it"—I recommend starting with Chapter 1 in Part One and working your way through.

TAKE THE QUIZ

Before jumping into the book, please take the **FREE 3-min "motivation type" quiz** and determine what is your motivation type. It will help you throughout this book. You can take the quiz at www.screwmotivationbook.com/quiz or by scanning the QR code below.

INVITATION

By purchasing this book, you have also received an accompanying **FREE Screw Motivation! 6-part online course.** You can get it by visiting www.screwmotivation book.com/freecourse or by scaning the QR code.

Become a Member of Screw Motivation Community

You can also become a part of the **Screw Motivation Community,** a place where we come together to support each other in building new habits and doing it when we don't feel like it. It's completely free, very interactive and you can join by visiting www.screwmotivationbook.com/community or by scanning the QR code.

Lastly, join our **Facebook group of Screw Motivators.** To join, you will be asked for a passcode, which is: "Screw motivation". You can join us by visiting www.facebook.com/ groups/scrwmotivation/ or by scanning the QR code.

WHY YOU DON'T NEED MOTIVATION (TO DO IT)

So how do you actually get yourself to "do it"? Do you really need motivation? Let's say you want to start going to the gym, exercise regularly, or maybe study more consistently. Or maybe you just want to feel more disciplined during the day—to get more done and make your time count. Do you actually need motivation to make it happen?

I hear people say it all the time: *"I'm just not motivated. I wish I had more motivation. I just don't feel like it."* But if you listen closely, what they're really saying is they *believe* they need to feel like it before they can do it. And that's the problem.

Because here's the truth: **you don't have to feel like it to do it.** Sure, it's nice if you do, and it does make the job easier, but it's not a must. Think about it: when you have to be at work at 8, you probably don't feel like going, but you still manage to get yourself there.

So, what's going on there?

Here's the real truth:

<u>Doing It"</u> Has Nothing to Do With <u>Feeling</u> Like It.

You don't have to feel like it to do it. You just have to do it. Easier said than done, I know. We all know we just need to get ourselves to do it... but how? Maybe we've tried a bunch of things, and they didn't work. We tried promising ourselves that *"tomorrow is the day,"* but then didn't do it so many times that we gave up on even saying it anymore.

So the question becomes—how do you actually make yourself do it, especially when you don't feel like it?

The first thing to understand is that **motivation is a misnomer.** It's not about motivation. You don't really need motivation to get yourself to follow through. Because the truth is motivation fluctuates. One day, it's there, and you feel like you can take on the world. The next day, it's gone, and you can't even get yourself off the couch.

Motivation is <u>unpredictable.</u> It's not something you can count on to be there when you need it.

It's like being in a relationship with a bipolar person—you never know who you're going to wake up to tomorrow. Will they be happy, sad, angry, or depressed? Motivation is just as unstable, and that's why you can't rely on it.

The real challenge isn't about motivation; it's about facing and dealing with *resistance*. This whole game is about overcoming resistance. Resistance is what you feel when it's time to do something you've committed to, and suddenly, every cell in your body doesn't want to do it. This is the real problem.

Think of a morning run you've promised yourself. You didn't overdo it by setting some crazy time like 4am—you just made a commitment to go for a run in the morning, after you wake up.

But then the day comes. You're rested, you have time, and you know this is what you really want to do. Yet there it is: resistance. You stand there, looking outside through your bedroom window, and running feels like the last thing you want to do. That's resistance in action.

So how do you go from standing in your room, staring out the window, to actually stepping outside and running? Or how do you get yourself to sit down and study when you said you'll study? Or get yourself do the work or write that report? How do you get yourself to do anything you've said you'll do?

That's what this book is here to help you with. By the time you finish, you'll know exactly how to get yourself out there—even when resistance is yelling at you to stay put.

The idea is simple: stop relying on motivation; focus on overcoming resistance. That's your real opponent. The goal isn't to "find motivation"; it's to break through resistance.

To get there, we'll first establish the foundation you need to confront it effectively. Because resistance often masks something deeper. When we procrastinate or "don't feel like it," it's usually because of one of these four things:

THE FOUR PROBLEMS

1. We haven't made a **real, genuine <u>decision</u>** to do it.
2. We don't **believe in our <u>ability</u>** to make it happen.
3. We don't feel <u>**worthy**</u> of achieving the goal.
4. We're <u>**afraid**</u>—of either **failure** or **success**.

This is what we're going to explore in this book.

Let's dive in.

WHERE DO YOU WANT TO GET YOURSELF TO "DO IT"?

Before you dive into the strategies in this book, take a moment to think about where do you struggle with getting yourself to "do it".

Is it exercising? Perhaps studying regularly? Maybe working on your business? Where do you wish you could get yourself to "do it," even when you don't feel like it?

Write it here:

____

____

____

____

Keep your goal in mind as you read through the book. It'll make all the difference as you focus on what's most important to you and make it easier to apply the ideas to your own life.

PART ONE
THE INVISIBLE FORCES

CHAPTER 1
THE FAT GUY IN THE MIRROR

A few years ago, I stepped out of the shower and caught my reflection in the mirror. There I was, weighing around 320 pounds (about 140 kilograms). Even for someone naturally heavier, this was too much.

My stomach sagged, my face was puffy, and my chest looked like I was breastfeeding. I couldn't believe my eyes. I thought, *"What the hell have I done to myself?"*

In that instant, I had a flashback to every piece of candy I put in my mouth, every midnight snack, every potato chip I mindlessly devoured while watching a movie on my couch.

I could clearly see how every decision I had made up to that point had brought me to this moment. It was all there: every skipped workout, every candy bar, every fast-food meal, every snack I told myself "didn't matter."

But now, staring at myself in the mirror, it was clear that it did matter.

That mirror moment was a turning point for me.

Disgusted and disappointed, I asked myself, *"What are you doing? How did you let things get this far?"*

And then – something clicked.

I made a decision.

I decided to change. I promised myself that I would never find myself in this situation again. This was more than a fleeting thought or a temporary feeling - it was a turning point. I didn't just wish to change, I <u>had</u> to change.

That decision, born out of frustration and a raw, honest look at myself, became my foundation.

I committed.

From that point on, I got to work. I started exercising regularly. I stopped eating junk and became mindful of the food I was putting into my body. If there was a piece of candy on the table, I would just ignore it instead of mindlessly reaching for it.

There were certainly days when I didn't feel like exercising. There were tempting moments when I was hungry, and I just wanted to grab something to eat quickly.

But resistance never got the best of me. It didn't matter whether I felt like it or not—I went and exercised. It didn't matter how tempted I was to eat junk food, I simply didn't do it. I didn't need motivation. I didn't need anyone cheering me on. <u>I just did it.</u>

So what changed? Why was I able to push through resistance, and resist temptation?

It was because I made a <u>real</u> decision.

A real, genuine decision was the foundation for everything else. From that point on, every step I took, every bit of resistance I faced, every time I didn't feel like it—I would always remember that moment in front of the mirror when I made the decision.

A Decision Is the Foundation

If you want to make yourself "do it", whatever that might be, if you're serious about breaking through the resistance that holds you back, you need one thing at the core: a real decision.

Not a half-hearted wish, not a vague "I should." It has to be the kind of decision that leaves no space for a way out. You're either in, or you're not.

For example, there are people out there who talk about how much they want to lose weight. They seem like they want it. But they don't really want it. Maybe you know the type—they're always on some new diet. Today it's Atkins, tomorrow it's Keto, and next week they're doing intermittent fasting. Then it's no sugar.

At first, they seem to have all the motivation and excitement to do it, but a week into it, they're back to their old habits, stuffing themselves with burgers and fries, forgetting all about their commitment. Then, a few months later, they're excitedly talking about yet another new diet they found online that they're going to "try."

It never works—they never lose weight. They always stay the same. Why? **Because they haven't really decided.** They're fooling themselves—and everyone around them. They say they want it, but they don't really mean it. Because when you truly want something, **you speak with your actions, not your words.**

Here's something I've learned in the past decade from working with hundreds of people all over the world:

People are where they are because that is <u>exactly</u> where they really want to be. If they wanted something different, they would <u>already</u> be doing it.

THIS IS a hard pill to swallow for many. But look at yourself—from your weight, to your finances, to your relationships, to your level of happiness—you are exactly where you want to be. If you wanted to be in a different position, you would either have already made it happen or be on your way to making it happen.

If you say you want to lose weight, but your actions say something else, it's because you don't actually want to lose weight. You're okay with where you are. You haven't really decided.

If you say you want to build a business but you're sleeping till noon, then no—you don't really want it. If you're in school but you keep putting off studying, you haven't really decided. If you'd actually made the decision, you'd study whether you felt like it or not.

Until you decide, you're wasting everyone's time—including your own. If you're not willing to really decide and commit, ask yourself why you're even pretending to want it in the first place? Why are you wasting your time playing half-hearted games with yourself?

THE POWER OF REASONS

To make a strong decision, one that would make you *do it* even if you don't feel like it, you have to have a compelling reason *why*.

In psychology, there's an expression that a strong decision will outweigh bad habits. But a weak decision will always be overpowered by those habits. What makes a decision strong? It's reasons. If you have strong reasons, then your decision will be strong. You won't need motivation. My decision came from seeing myself in the mirror. So every time I didn't "feel like it", I'd just remember that image.

A few years ago, I followed a guy on YouTube on his journey of losing weight. Let me say, he started out extremely overweight—you know, the kind where it changes the shape of your eyes. I honestly had my doubts about whether or not he could do it. Yet, to my surprise, he stayed committed and actually lost the weight.

What stuck with me the most was when I heard him talk about his reasons for his decision to lose weight.

He said, *"I wanted to be able to play with my kids. I wanted to run with them and not get tired."* And that was it—clear, concise, simple. No "It would be nice" or "I'll try." He knew exactly why he wanted to lose weight.

Now, don't get me wrong. Even with that commitment, his path wasn't just a straight road up. There were days he felt like quitting, days he doubted himself, days he felt ridiculous for even trying. But his *decision* made him able to push through resistance and *do it* no matter how he felt.

That's the power of a strong reason.

MOST PEOPLE NEVER ACTUALLY DECIDE

Most people never actually decide. They think they want change, they talk about it, they make plans, but none of that is a real decision. A decision means you've had it. It means you mean it. It means you have *decided* to go through it, no matter what.

Think about the goals you've set in the past. Maybe it was to lose weight, to get in shape, to start a business, or to do well in school.

How many of those goals faded out the moment things got uncomfortable, the moment you didn't *feel* like it? Be honest with yourself: did you really decide to do them? Because if you had, you'd have stuck to it even on the days you felt zero motivation.

A decision isn't easy. It requires you to say, "This is what I'm doing. Period." There's often a cost to it – letting go of comfort of doing whatever you want, the comfort of staying the same – but that is exactly why it has so much power.

You look at everything you have to "lose" by making that decision and still move forward with it, because the reason behind it is far more important than the comfort you're currently experiencing.

SCREW MOTIVATION!

If you're waiting for motivation to get started, to "feel like it", you may be waiting for a long time. Because it may never come. Real change doesn't come from motivation; it comes from a <u>decision</u>.

We're constantly fed this idea that we need to feel motivated to act. But as we said, motivation is very fleeting. It fluctuates – one day it's here, the next day it's gone.

How do you know how you'll feel tomorrow?

Will you wake up happy, sad, motivated to exercise or feel like you just want to stay in bed all day?

The moment you start relying on your feelings to do the things you want to do, <u>you have already lost.</u>

You have to do it *despite* your feelings.

Let me say this again: **you don't need motivation to make yourself do it.** You need something that doesn't depend on your mood, that doesn't care how you're feeling on a particular day. That's what a <u>decision</u> is.

The whole game is about overcoming *resistance*. How do you make yourself "do it" on days when you're tired, when you're overwhelmed, when everything in you wants to stop? A decision will give you the strength to push through all that resistance. Every time you hit that wall, every time you don't feel like it, that decision will remind you why you're doing it in the first place.

You don't make a decision just once and then forget about it. A real decision is something you come back to over and over, especially when it's starts feeling hard. When resistance shows up, when your excuses start sounding good, and you feel like drifting away, your decision becomes your anchor, keeping you firm on the path you've chosen.

For example, **even though my decision to get and stay in shape was strong, I still faced resistance.** There were numerous days where I didn't feel like going for that run because it was cold outside and so warm inside. But just one second of remembering myself standing in front of that mirror helped me push through any resistance I felt in the moment.

If you've decided, you won't let the resistance stop you. You'll get up, push through, and you'll do. That's how "doing it" happens—not because it's easy or because you feel like it, but because you made a decision.

MAKE A DECISION

Imagine every area in your life where you're falling short. Your health, fitness, your relationships, money, school, business, whatever it is. Look at each one honestly and ask yourself if you've actually decided to make that area successful?

Everything in this book—every technique, every strategy, every method for overcoming resistance—comes back to this one thing: a <u>decision</u>. Not a wish, not an idea, not a vague intention. A decision to act, whether you feel like it or not.

If you're reading this and you're waiting for motivation, stop. If you're looking for the right mood, let it go. You're in control of one thing right now, and that's making a decision.

- **Is it in your business**—committed one day, drifting back to half-measures the next, never truly committing?
- **Is it in your studies**—motivated and driven one day, then 'doom scrolling' social media the next?
- **Maybe in your fitness**—you get in shape for a month, only to let it slide the next?

What would it take for you to draw a line in the sand and say, *enough is enough—I'm done with dabbling*? When will you decide you've had it?

Imagine your life if you truly made that decision today. How would things change if you stopped waiting and went all in? Would it be easier? Harder? Worth it? The choice is yours. If you're not going to decide, at least stop playing games with yourself and others. Stop saying you'll "do it one day" and get real.

Look in the mirror—literally, if you need to—and ask yourself: *Are you truly serious about what you say you want?* Decide, commit fully —no backup plan, no safety net—and start now.

CHAPTER 2
MAKE THE FIRE BURN

Remember what we said in the previous chapter – a strong decision will outweigh a weak habit, but a weak decision will be overrun by a stronger habit.

The question then is, how do you make that strong decision? Everybody can "know" that they need to decide, but how do you actually do it?

Imagine a scale in your mind. This scale measures how you feel about doing anything. On one side of the scale, you have all the reasons for doing something. And on the other side of the scale you have all the reasons against doing something.

Whichever side has more reasons, that's where the scale will tip – and that's how you'll decide.

So to make any kind of a decision, you have to start by asking yourself about your reasons – why? Why do you want it?

If you want to lose weight, why is that important to you? What will you gain if you do? What will it cost you if you don't?

If you want to build a business – why do you want to do it?

If you want to study more regularly – why? Why is it important to you? What would you gain if you did that? What would you avoid from happening?

Why Reasons Matter

For a decision to be strong, it has to have a strong reason or reasons. Without it, your decision will fall apart as soon as things get hard. You'll eat that cookie; you'll scroll social media instead of studying and you'll procrastinate on working on your business.

But if your reasons are strong, and you have a lot of them, now you'll have something that pushes you through resistance even on days when you really don't feel like doing it.

Sometimes, a single reason is enough to drive you forward. Other times, it's about stacking up a bunch of reasons—little and big— until they add up to a strong decision.

Imagine each reason you find is like adding a log to a fire. With just a few logs, the fire burns out quickly. But if you keep stacking log after log, you build a fire that's strong and steady, one that won't go out easily. When you stack up reasons they make your decision solid, keeping you going even when things get tough.

Find the Big, Personal Reasons

Let's start with the big reasons—the ones that mean something to you personally. These are the reasons tied to who you are, what you care about, or the people you love. These are the reasons that hit home, that feel hard to ignore or walk away from.

Ask yourself: Why do I even want this? Why am I doing it?

Let's say you want to lose weight or get in shape. But why? What's the point? Is it just to look better? Or is there more to it? If you dig deeper, you might realize that it's not just about the weight. Maybe it's about feeling confident again, setting an example for your kids, or just feeling like you're in control of your own life.

Remember our Youtuber who decided to lose weight so he could play with his kids and not get tired? These kinds of reasons have power. They're the ones that don't fade easily and that actually make it feel like you have to follow through. It's hard to walk away from something that's tied to your core values or to the people you care about most.

The Power of a Big Reason

I remember a friend who tried to quit smoking several times, but he always failed because his reasons weren't strong enough. He was doing it because he "should" or because other people wanted him to. He thought he wanted it, but when push came to shove, it was easy for him to slip back into the habit.

Then, his first child was born. He didn't want to be the dad who had to step outside every hour for a smoke or the one who wasn't around because of a health issue. Suddenly, his reason was real. He wasn't quitting because he felt like he should; he was quitting because really wanted to. He wanted to be the kind of father he could feel proud of. That reason stuck. It became stronger than the cravings or the habit, and he quit cold turkey and never looked back.

Sometimes, all it takes is one big reason like that to keep you going. If it's tied to something real in your life, you'll have an easier time sticking to it.

SOMETIMES, one big reason might not feel enough. In those cases, think of stacking up different types of reasons. Motivations often come from different sources—each has its own strengths. Here are the four categories to consider when finding your reasons:

1. External Negative Reasons

These are reasons based on avoiding something negative. Maybe you're trying to avoid a consequence or prevent something bad from happening. For example, maybe you want to exercise because you don't want to show an out-of-shape body on the beach, or maybe you're motivated to study because you don't want to fail a class.

While these reasons can work in the short term, they might not be strong enough on their own. Because what happens when the summer is over or you don't have an exam coming up? External negative reasons are often tied to fear or discomfort, which might push you to act at first but won't always last.

2. External Positive Reasons

External positive reasons are about chasing something you want or something you'll get as a reward. For example, you might be motivated to get in shape so that other people can admire your body on the beach, or maybe you're working hard at school because you want praise from your teachers or parents.

I have a collection of shirts that only fit me if I'm in shape. If I gain weight, they don't fit anymore. So when I don't feel like exercising, I think about how those shirts will fit, and sometimes that gives me the extra push I need to get moving.

This kind of motivation is better than negative, but it's still based on something outside yourself. External positive reasons can help, but once you get the reward, that fire may fade.

3. Internal Negative Reasons

Internal negative reasons come from within but are based on avoiding feelings like guilt or self-criticism. For example, you might work out because you hate the way you look, or you study hard because you don't want to feel like a failure.

While internal negative reasons can motivate you to take action, they often come with a negative self-image. It's like pushing yourself to change because you don't like yourself as you are. The issue with this approach is that it's a goal you can never fully reach because the "carrot" keeps moving. This mindset can eventually lead to burnout or general unhappiness with yourself.

4. Internal Positive Reasons

This is the strongest and healthiest base for a strong decision—internal positive reasons are about doing something because you genuinely want to do it. You study because you want to become a doctor, a lawyer, an engineer, or simply be a person with a degree. You exercise because you like how it makes you feel afterwards and it aligns with your values, your identity, and who you want to be.

This is about wanting to grow or improve yourself <u>for yourself</u> – not because someone else expects it, or because you're trying to prove something to others, or avoid something.

Internal positive reasons stick because they're based on who you are, who you want to be and what you care about deeply. These are the reasons that don't fade because they're part of you.

Although the internal positive motivation is the healthiest foundation for a decision, the truth is, you can use whatever motivation you need to get started. If you want to get fit for the summer and that's what drives you, then go ahead. If getting good grades to earn praise or admiration from others is what fuels you, use that too. The key is to use whatever motivation gets you moving — but here's the key: don't stay there. Keep developing your reasons as you progress.

For example, maybe you start exercising just to get in shape for the summer, but as you continue, you might discover other reasons. Maybe you find that you enjoy the workouts, you're in a better mood when you do them, and your skin is glowing. Eventually, you might realize that this is simply who you want to be.

Exercise: Finding Your Reasons

Now take a look at each of the 4 categories and find reasons within them. Some goals will benefit from a combination of reasons, while others may rely more heavily on one type.

For example, when trying to get in shape, you may find that you have a mix of motivations:

External negative reasons (avoiding looking bad), external positive reasons (fitting into new clothes or having the beach body), internal negative reasons (avoiding feelings of regret), and powerful internal positive reasons (feeling strong, confident and proud of yourself).

Now, let's get started.

Think about something you want to do, be it get in shape, study, start a business or take your business to the next level…

Think about why you want it.

1. **First, write the external negative reasons.** What's going
   to happen if you don't get in shape, if you don't study, or if
   you don't take your business to the next level?

What are all the ways that will cost you? What will you miss out on?
Maybe you won't be able to play with your kids without getting
tired. Maybe you'll get bad grades and won't be able to get that
dream job you want. Maybe you won't achieve that financial goal
you set for yourself? Think of all the ways that not having that goal is
going to cost you.

____

____

____

____

____

2. **Second, write the external positive reasons.** What will
   you gain if you do it? If you study regularly? If you work
   out and get in shape? If you take your business to the next
   level? What possibilities will be available to you now? Will
   your kids like you more? Will you have more money? Will
   other people praise you and admire you?

____

____

____

____

____

3. **Third, write the internal negative reasons.** How will
   you feel if you don't do it? Maybe you'll think less of
   yourself or won't feel as proud of yourself as you would.

Maybe you'll feel like a failure. Maybe you'll feel like you've let yourself and others down.

____
____
____
____
____

4. **Fourth, write the internal positive reasons.** How will you feel if you do it? Will you feel proud of yourself? Will you feel accomplished and more worthy? For example, every time I complete my run, I feel on top of the world. I feel like I can deal with any problem or any situation life offers me.

How would you feel if you did what you say you will do? If you studied on time – how would yo u feel afterwards? If you stayed focused and was very productive in your work – how would you feel at the end of the day? If you completed your workout – how would you feel?

____
____
____
____

Keep Your Reasons Close

Once you've found your reasons, keep them close. Don't just come up with them once and forget about them. Write them down somewhere you can see them every day. Remind yourself of them whenever things feel hard or when you start doubting if it's worth it.

- **Keep your list of reasons somewhere visible.** Whether it's on your phone, on a sticky note, or in a notebook, seeing your reasons often helps make them real.
- **Add new reasons as you go.** Your reasons can grow and change over time, and that's a good thing. The more reasons you find, the stronger your commitment gets.

When you look at your reasons every day, they start to feel like a part of you. It doesn't feel like you're forcing yourself—you're just following through on something that matters.

Be Honest About Weak Reasons

Not all reasons are equal. Sometimes, we come up with reasons that sound good but don't actually mean much. If a reason doesn't feel real or important, it's probably not going to help when things get hard.

Ask yourself if each reason you've come up with feels **real**. Are you doing it for you, or are you just telling yourself you "should"? If a reason feels weak, let it go, and focus on the ones that matter to you.

For example, if you have a reason of " I'll feel good", that's probably not going to hold. You may want to dig deeper, what is your reason for doing it? Once you do, you may find a better reason, like, "I will finally be able to look at myself in the mirror and feel like that I am becoming the person I always wanted to become..."

Build a Foundation

The stronger and clearer your reasons are, the more powerful your decision becomes. For some goals, one big reason might be all you need. For others, you might need a stack of smaller ones. But whatever it takes, make sure you have enough reasons to keep you grounded.

So build a foundation for your decision based on reasons. Ask yourself: What are my reasons? What makes this decision feel unbreakable?

And as you go forward, keep your reasons close. When you face resistance, when you don't feel like doing it, remember why you started. Let your reasons carry you through.

CHAPTER 3
"BUT I'M NOT WORTHY"

You've made a decision, you've found your "why," and you're ready to take action. But then, just when it's time to take that step—whether it's running, studying, or working on a business—you feel something holding you back. Maybe you brush it off as laziness or think it's a lack of discipline, but often, it's something deeper.

What's really happening is your limiting identity holding you back. Your identity is the story you tell yourself about who you are and who you're not. How much you're worth and how much you deserve. If that doesn't align with your goals, you're going to feel resistance to it without knowing why.

Resistance Isn't Just About Discipline

Imagine you decide to start working out. At first, you're all in. But then you start finding reasons not to go—"I'll go tomorrow," or "It's too cold." Often, what's really going on beneath these excuses, is a quiet voice saying, "Maybe I'm not really the kind of person who gets fit. Who am I kidding? This isn't who I really AM..." That voice is your identity trying to keep you in the role that you feel you deserve, even if it's not where you want to be.

In 1960, a plastic surgeon named Maxwell Maltz wrote a book called PsychoCybernetics, about a concept he called self-image. He noticed that after performing cosmetic procedures on his patients, such as giving them a new nose, some felt more confident and surer of themselves. However, he also noticed that when he did the same procedure on others, they felt no change in how they saw themselves. So, even though they got a new nose, a facelift, or some other change, they still felt the same—unattractive and insecure.

He found that we have two images—one external and one internal—and that an internal self-image doesn't always change with external changes. And this right here—your internal image of how you see yourself—is the main problem.

Because if you see yourself as X and would like to become Y, but you don't see yourself as a person who deserves to have Y, you will sabotage your efforts.

For example, if want to get in shape, but inside you see yourself as an "overweight" person, when you start working out, you may start feeling weird about it. Almost like you are doing something you *shouldn't* do because it doesn't feel like *you*.

Or if you see yourself as a person who doesn't have a lot of money and you get into business – you will probably carry your poor money identity with you and struggle. Making money will feel like it's not *you*.

The Power of a Limiting "You"

Your sense of who "you" are can act like an invisible wall, keeping you within where you feel you really "belong" and where your "place" is. Once you take on a role—whether it's the "struggling student," the "average earner," or the "out-of-shape person"—you subconsciously act in ways that match it. Even if you say you want something different, that identity will hold you back from doing what it takes to get it.

For instance, when I was working in sales, I never made more than $1500 a month, while many of my peers were earning $5k, $10k, or even $15k. Even though I tried everything to break through that limit, I stayed stuck at $1500. Why? Because my parents had never earned more than that, I subconsciously believed that was where I belonged. My identity—the idea of being part of a "$1500 family"—held me back. Nobody told me this was "our" limit; I just accepted it without questioning.

I once worked with a client who struggled to make his business stable. Even though he was doing all the "right" things, he kept having the same issues. He would have a great month or two, followed by a stagnation and bad months. He couldn't figure it out.

When we started working together, we went deeper and found the cause: his limiting identity. He saw himself as someone who only made a certain amount of money. Once his business reached that threshold, he acted like a thermostat, automatically shutting himself off. He stopped doing the right things, and gradually, his business slipped back to a level where he felt comfortable. But when his income fell below that point, he would turn back on and start working again.

This is our limiting identity at work. It keeps us below what we could really do and be, but just above where we don't completely sink.

Once we changed how he saw himself, he stopped sabotaging himself and was able to break through those limits and reach stability in both business and life.

For example:

- **Procrastination** – putting off tasks, not because you're lazy, but because you doubt you'll succeed, so you rather delay than face the possibility of failing.
- **Self-Sabotage** – doing things that push you further from your goal, like eating junk food when you're trying to get healthy, or ignoring deadlines even when you have time.
- **Overthinking** – getting stuck in planning and analysis, learning, taking courses and reading books but never taking action.
- **Imposter Syndrome** – Feeling like you are just "playing pretend" and that people are going to find out you are fake. Really not believing in yourself and that what you are trying to do will work.

If you're struggling to take action, ask yourself if it's really about "not feeling like it" or if it's the result of that old belief whispering, "This isn't for me." Because more often than not, you're just reacting to the limits you've put on yourself a long time ago.

Guilt and Feeling "Undeserving"

Here's an interesting phenomenon I've noticed. Sometimes, people's limits come not from lack but from having too much. I've worked with a few clients that were born into wealth, and they weren't sure how to deal with it.

Because of it, they felt guilty and undeserving. They thought they've had it easier than others and questioned their own worth to go and create success on their own.

Often, I would see them pull back, not give their best because they always felt guilty. Guilt can act like a weight, pulling you back even more forcefully than a sense of lack.

But what good does that do? What good does it do to hold yourself back and not use what you have? Does it turn a poor person rich? Does it stop a war? Does it make someone feel better? It does none of that. Keeping yourself small doesn't help anyone.

You need to get rid of guilt and run with what you have. <u>Everyone is dealt a different hand in life</u>. If you were born into wealth, great! Use it! Don't sit on the guilt trip. Instead of feeling guilty, consider how you could use what you've got. Imagine the positive impact you could make. Ask yourself, what can you do with the advantages you have?

HOW OUR LIMITING IDENTITY FORMS

Much of what you believe about yourself started early in life. Every little comment or reaction, all the ideas people had about you—they all helped build up a picture of who you thought you were. Those early beliefs, the limits you thought you had, and even what you thought you deserved, were formed by others, not by you.

Let's say you come from a family of mechanics. It's in the blood: your dad, brothers, uncles—all mechanics. Now imagine you decide you want to be a business person, or maybe a stockbroker in New York. How would you feel? Probably out of place. You'd think to yourself, "*Who am I to do this?*" You would probably feel that pull, that pressure to stay in line with what's "normal," for you. So, what do you do? Do you go for that new career, or do you stay "loyal" to your family business?

I had a client who was very successful in her corporate work but wanted to transition to becoming a full-time life coach. She loved it and felt that this was her destiny.

However, despite putting in a lot of effort, time, and money, she never seemed to make significant progress. The reason? She was being held back by a limiting identity.

She simply saw herself as an employee at a big corporation, not as an entrepreneur. She believed that people make a living in high-paying jobs, not by running a business in something as vague as coaching.

Think about how were you influenced? Are you still limiting yourself in some ways, and you're not sure why?

Maybe your parents told you that money was tight, or you grew up seeing people struggle to get by. Even if no one said it outright, you might have absorbed the idea that "people like us don't get rich."

If you grew up with people who believed in you, who told you that you were smart, talented, or capable, then those beliefs might have helped you feel worthy and capable. But for many people, it's the limiting ideas, the doubts, and the quiet whispers of "not good enough" that seem to sink in the hardest.

Even our level of happiness can be tied to how we see ourselves, which is often shaped by what we were taught growing up. If we were raised in an environment where happiness was limited or restrained, we may unconsciously believe we're only allowed to feel a certain amount of happiness. As a result, we'll keep ourselves at that same level, never allowing ourselves to feel any happier than what we were taught was "normal" in our home.

The fact is, our limiting identity is a result of what we were told we were from other people – parents, teachers, peers, siblings, environment, etc. And sometimes it's not even verbal, but happens on a subconscious level.

THE FLEAS IN A JAR EXPERIMENT

Scientists did an interesting experiment with fleas. They placed a group of fleas in a jar and closed it with a lid. At first, the fleas tried to jump high, but when they hit the lid, they learned to only jump to that limit. After some time, the scientists took off the lid, but the fleas still jumped only to the height the lid used to be. Even when he put them out of the jar and on a table, they kept jumping only <u>as high as they had learned to jump while in the jar.</u>

But here's the kicker: this limit didn't just affect the adult fleas; it also passed down to their babies. When the fleas had babies, even though the babies were never in the jar, they still jumped to the same height as their parents.

This shows how our idea about who we think we are is transferred from our environment, and acts as a "lid" to our potential.

(By the way, if you'd like to see this in action, go on youtube and type in "fleas in a jar experiment" to see it.)

Sometimes we <u>think</u> we lack motivation, that we can't get ourselves to take action, or that we fall into patterns like yo-yo dieting or self-sabotage. But in reality, it's our limiting identity at play, quietly shaping our behavior based on who we think we are and how much we deserve.

If you think/feel that you belong in a certain place, you will stay there. **If you see yourself as an overweight person** and you fundamentally believe that that's where you belong, you will <u>stay over-</u>

<u>weight</u>. You won't have motivation to exercise or to keep an eye on your diet.

If you see yourself as an unsuccessful person, and you fundamentally believe that you don't deserve to be successful, and that success isn't for people like "you", you will <u>not</u> create success. You will stay the same. You will procrastinate on doing what you need to do, distract yourself or literally sabotage your own progress.

If you want to move forward, you have to get rid of these beliefs about who you are, what you deserve and where you belong. You have to "clear your plate" and realize that you are no different than anyone else in this world, and that you deserve just as much as anyone.

The truth is, you aren't rooted by anything. Every single person in your family could be a mechanic, and you can still go for that job in New York. You could be coming from a poor background and still create success and wealth for yourself. You could be overweight your entire life, but could lose weight and get fit in 6 months, if you just choose to. You aren't limited by anything. The limits we feel are rarely about the reality of what we can do; they're about how familiar or "normal" it feels to us.

So Ask Yourself...

- Who do you believe you **are**?
- What do you believe you **deserve**?
- And where is it all **coming from**?

In health and fitness, who are you? How do you see yourself? Do you see yourself as an overweight or a fit person? What do you think and feel are your fitness limits? Where is it coming from? Are you sure you couldn't be anything more?

In business, how do you see yourself? Do you see yourself being at the level of successful people, or are you stuck in an identity that is limiting you? Maybe you feel like an imposter, like you don't really deserve to do what you are trying to do?

With money, how do you see yourself? Are you a person who always struggles with money, or are you someone who always has money? How do you think money feels to people like you? Are you someone who deserves money?

How do you see yourself in relationships? Are you someone that people want to have a relationship with? Do you see yourself as someone who can't keep a relationship? Maybe you see yourself as someone who isn't attractive or interesting to other people. What do you believe your "relationship destiny" is?

<u>Now challenge it.</u>

If your identity is limiting, challenge its presumptions. Ask yourself, is that really true? Could something else be true? Is it really true that I cannot be what I want to be? Am I really destined for defeat? Is there an example in the real world where I can see something else?

There's a lot of power in reasoning with yourself. Often, we can be convinced that we are limited in a certain way, but when we question where that came from and why we think the way we do, we often find out that our beliefs are based on shaky foundations.

For example, **I may believe I am destined to be overweight** because I've always been that way. But if I go online and see examples of people who were overweight just like me, and then managed to lose weight and get fit, it may loosen my belief about what I can do.

You may believe you can't really make that business work because that isn't "you", or that you don't deserve it, but then see a lot of people like you (or even less smart than you) doing the very thing you would like to do.

You may believe that you can't make relationships work because of failed relationships you had in the past, but when you question it, you may find out your limiting beliefs about yourself are the real problem.

THE HANDSOMELY UNATTRACTIVE

I once worked with a guy who couldn't make his relationships work. He was looking to find a partner to marry, but despite being fairly good looking, he struggled to attract women. At first, there was initial attraction, but soon women would lose interest. This puzzled me because on the outside, he seemed like he had it all – successful, handsome, well-travelled and all in all a very rounded, interesting person.

But as we dug deeper, the real issue became clear: **he had a limiting identity**. When he was a kid, he was chubby, and girls never showed interest in him. They would often tease him, making him feel unattractive. Even though he had grown into a successful, handsome man, he still saw himself as that chubby kid who women aren't interested in. When talking to women, he felt they would soon discover that he wasn't really interesting—and, that's exactly what happened.

I asked him to reflect on and challenge the beliefs from his past. Was he really still that chubby kid? Would women really not find him interesting? As he began to understand where these beliefs came from, he was able to loosen them. Slowly, he started seeing himself as the confident, interesting man, and he became more confident around women. A few months later, he sent me a message saying he was in a new relationship, and soon after, he got married.

Ask yourself: Why do I believe this? Was there an event in my past that led me to form this belief? Did someone tell me? Did I observe it? How did I decide who I was, what I was worth, where I belong, and where my limits lie?

As you begin this process, you'll start to realize that many of the limits you've set for yourself were decided a long time ago—and they're probably not true anymore. Your limiting identity will gradually loosen its grip, allowing new beliefs about who you are to take root and grow.

How Would the New You Look Like?

Recently I was listening to a podcast with a bodybuilder, who shared the story of his transformation. He said that at some point in his life, he simply got curious – he wanted to know how it would feel to live with muscles. How it would feel to go wash his car with muscles, do grocery shopping with muscles, talk with people with muscles, etc. He placed that new version of himself in the real world until it became a reality.

Whenever you go about your day, ask yourself: **How would the new version of me act in this situation?** If you want to be fit, how would a fit version of you handle lunch or a workout?

If you want to be successful, how would a successful version of you do the thing you're about to do? If you were a straight A student, how would you approach your studies? If you were a confident and attractive person, how would you behave with the person you want to date?

Don't overthink it—just keep this idea in your mind. The more you start seeing yourself as this new person, the more it will feel normal, and the more you'll naturally act like it.

It doesn't have to be some huge transformation overnight. It's about taking small steps that match who you want to be. Each time you act in line with this new identity, it chips away at the old one. You're not "pretending"—you're creating something new.

You Deserve the Life You Want

Yes, it sounds cheesy. It sounds so self-helpy. But there is no better way to put it. Here's the bottom line: you deserve the life you want. It doesn't matter where you came from, what your past experiences were, or what you used to believe.

Decide who you're going to be going forward. Make a decision that you're going to show up as the person you want to be, not the person you've been told to be.

Ask yourself: What kind of life would you build if you stopped worrying about who you're "supposed" to be? What could you achieve if you didn't hold yourself back?

It's up to you. The choice is yours. All you have to do is decide—and then act on it, every single day.

CHAPTER 4
"BUT I CAN'T DO IT"

There's another thing that covers up as resistance:

DOUBT.

Doubt is sneaky. It doesn't walk up to you openly; it slides in, quietly making you question your ability to pull off the things you want. We often mistake it for something else. Maybe we think we just don't feel like working on a goal, or we keep finding excuses to push it off for "later." But when you dig deeper, you'll see what's really going on: *doubt*.

Specifically, it's the kind of doubt that says, "You're not capable of this." Once you've made a decision to pursue something — whether it's to get fit, start a business, or learn a new skill — doubt shows up with a whisper: *"Sure, but can you really do this?"*

Take the example of getting in shape when you've been overweight for years. If that's been your story, the doubt might sound something like, *"I've never been fit in my life, so what makes me think I can do it now?"* Or say you're aiming to build a business. You've made the decision, but in the back of your mind, you're asking yourself, *"Do I actually have what it takes? Will it really work?"*

So let's break this down: What is doubt really made of? Why does it come up?

After working with so many people and going through my own struggles, I've found that **doubt boils down to two big obstacles:**

1. Avoiding _Complexity_
2. Fear of _Effort and Work_

Let's take a closer look at both.

1. COMPLEXITY

First up, **complexity**. Complexity spooks us. There's something about looking at a new task, skill, or goal that makes the brain say, *"No way can I handle this."* You know the feeling: you're staring at something you've never done before, and it looks like a tangled mess with no clear beginning or end. Complexity can overwhelm you in seconds, and when that happens, doubt sets in fast.

Think about it: you open a new piece of software, crack open a dense textbook, or even try putting together a piece of IKEA furniture. There are a hundred of parts, a jumble of information, and it looks like absolute chaos. Complexity makes you feel like you're staring up at a wall that's way too high to climb. And so, instead of beginning, you back off, telling yourself, "Maybe later," or "It's not for me."

But here's the truth: **complexity itself isn't the problem.** The real problem is letting it scare you off. Complexity is just information that hasn't been broken down yet. And once you start breaking it down, complexity starts to lose its power.

Let's go back to that IKEA closet example. Maybe you tried putting it together at least once in your life? What happens? You open the boxes and dump all the pieces on the floor, and it's a mess — no order, just parts everywhere. But if you stop and open the instruction manual, and start with one screw, one board, piece by piece, it stops feeling so overwhelming. By the time you're 30 minutes in, the closet is starting to take shape. That overwhelming mess is turning into a closet you can use.

It's the same with any goal.

In my university, there was a notoriously difficult math exam that 70% of students failed on their first attempt. When I saw it, I was sure I'd never pass it. It looked so complex and intimidating, and that doubt kicked in, telling me to back off. But because it was one of the final exams to get my degree, I simply HAD to pass it.

So I got a tutor, dedicated two weeks to studying, and got on it. At first, I was overwhelmed. I didn't even know what I was looking at. But as I kept at it, that complexity broke down piece by piece, and I slowly started figuring it out. In the end, I passed the exam.

Your brain is capable of way more than you think. If you can make yourself to sit with a problem for just 20 minutes, focusing on it, you'll find your brain starts piecing things together. Marie Forleo has a saying I really like – *Everything is Figureoutable*. And I think it hits it on the head. That's the whole concept — everything is *figureoutable*, no matter how complex it looks at first.

So why do we avoid complexity? Why do we fear it? Why do we doubt our ability to figure out something complex, just because it's complex? Driving a car is complex, yet a lot of people do it. Using a computer is also complex, but most of us use it.

There's an interesting concept called Cognitive Load Theory that says that when our brain gets overloaded, it simply shuts down. It's the brain's way of saying, 'This is too much for now, bye!' But the thing is that when we start learning anything, everything feels like it's too much. The "overloading" is how learning starts. At first, nothing makes sense – but then the pieces start falling into place and you start to "get it".

Look at Elon Musk. He didn't start out as a trained rocket scientist, yet he founded SpaceX, a company that builds actual rockets. Musk famously said, *"You can learn anything you want if you're willing to ask enough questions and learn."*

When he decided to get into space technology, he didn't know anything about space engineering. But instead of getting spooked by complexity – after all, it was rocket science – he faced it. He delved into books, articles, and spoke with experts willing to share their knowledge. He started with the book *Rocket Propulsion Elements* by George Sutton, and took it from there.

He transformed himself in a learning machine, determined to understand everything from the basic principles to the most complex details.

And he figured it out.

I know you're not Elon Musk, but you're also not trying to figure out rocket science (or maybe you do?). Maybe your goal is to lose weight and stay in shape. Maybe to start or scale your business, or to study regularly for your exams.

If he was able to figure out rocket science, are you sure you can't figure out whatever it is you are trying to do? What are you procrastinating on and delaying because you're afraid you won't be able to figure it out?

Now let's talk about the second thing that fuels doubt: **fear of how much effort is it going to take.** Complexity is one thing, but even if we know how to break things down, there's often a lingering question: *"How much time and effort is this really going to take?"* It's a question that can make anyone hesitate, especially in a world that tells us everything should be fast and easy.

When you think about putting in effort, there's this strange fear that you'll have nothing left for anything else. Like somehow you think that the energy you put into a task will drain you dry.

Imagine if someone told you that there was gold buried in your backyard, and they had 100% proof that it's there. Would you dig for it? Would you be willing to put in the time and effort into it? And let's say you wouldn't find it immediately; how long would it take you to stop? Would you stop digging after an hour, a day, a week? Or would you keep going? How about if there was only a 50% chance that the gold was down there and you weren't so sure? Would you still put in the same amount of time? Or would you call it quits earlier? You might start, but after some time, you'd likely question whether it was worth the effort and give up.

This is a perfect example of why we avoid putting in the effort and time – because we are **uncertain** of the outcome. In other words, we aren't sure it's going to work. In psychology, this is called **uncertainty aversion** — our natural discomfort with ambiguity and lack of certainty. When outcomes are uncertain, we don't feel as compelled to put in the effort and work because we may not get anything for it.

However, here's what I've discovered: when you put in effort and work into something, even if you don't succeed, you often get a secondary benefit from it. For example, someone may try to become a football player, put in a lot of effort and work, but at the end not succeed. But all that effort does not go in vain. They can use that experience to become a football coach, or they can use what they've learned about team play and apply it in business. Effort and work never go to waste.

Think about working out: the more you exercise, the more energy you have. It doesn't drain you; it builds you up. And it's the same with effort. The more effort you invest in something, the more willpower you create. Effort is not a finite resource – it's something that grows the more you use it. Just like a muscle – the more you use it, the more it grows.

But let's talk about the elephant in the room:

LAZINESS.

After working with hundreds of people from all across the world, I can with certainty say that laziness is real human trait. We are all, at least to some degree, a little lazy.

And that's okay.

It's human nature to want to avoid what's hard, and instead to search for an easier way. And I don't have a problem with this. In fact, Bill Gates famously said that if he has a difficult task, he will give it to a lazy person – because they will always find an easier way to do it.

However, when you habitually look for an easier way, **you tend to start doubting your ability** to achieve goals.

Here's something I've learned:

THE LESS YOU ARE WILLING TO DO THE WORK, AND LOOK FOR SHORTCUTS, THE MORE YOU'RE GOING TO DOUBT YOUR ABILITY TO DO THINGS.

And likewise, the more you are willing to get to work, to waste no time and to jump into a task, the more confident you become in your ability to make things happen.

All it takes is facing complexity and putting in the work.

When you don't concern yourself with how much time something will take, how much effort and how much resources, you simply become more able to figure things out and achieve anything you want.

For over 5 years, I've been wanting to build a website in Word-Press. Every time I tried; it seemed ridiculously complex. I didn't consider myself a "tech guy" at all, so every time I opened up Word-Press, I felt like I was on another planet. It was intimidating and felt like way too much effort.

But one day, I decided I want to figure it out. I went on YouTube, searched for "how to make a WordPress website," clicked on the first video, and started following along. At first, nothing made sense. It all seemed so complex. And if I am honest, a thought did cross my mind that I want to quit and go do something else. But by that time, I understood the principle of learning, so I stuck with it. I didn't let myself get spooked by complexity and trusted I'll figure it out.

Well, sure enough, after just a couple of hours, I had a working website. Within two weeks, I'd mastered the basics of WordPress to the point that I could build sites for others if I wanted to. That effort I'd been afraid of? It paid me back in skills, confidence, and momentum. (You can check out my masterpiece at www.coachomir.com)

BECOME A LEARNING MACHINE

Now, here's where I want to take this. There's a concept Charlie Munger talks about: *becoming a learning machine*. Learning, according to Munger, is your true superpower. You don't need some physical advantage or natural talent. Learning is the one edge every human has. Yet, so many of us have bought into the myth that learning is only for "smart" people.

Figuring things out isn't reserved for geniuses. Anyone can learn if they are willing to face complexity instead of running from it, and put in the effort and time into it. Trust me, **it's not that hard.** Your brain is able to connect the dots, even if it seems like you'll never be able to figure it out. Trust yourself. Whatever it is, if you simply stay there for long enough, your brain will start putting the pieces together.

STEPS TO MASTERING COMPLEXITY

To truly become a "learning machine" like Elon Musk, there's a clear set of steps you need to follow. Learning isn't just about studying hard or reading books; it's a mindset of openness to learning, willingness to humble yourself, have that curious mind and eventually figure it out.

Here are the steps:

1. Face the Idea Instead of Running from It

The first step is to face what you want to learn head-on. Most people run away at the first sign of difficulty, labeling a topic or skill as "not for me" before they even begin. But if you really want to figure something out, you can't turn away when it feels intimidating or overwhelming. You need to consciously decide to face the complexity, acknowledge that it's challenging, but not impossible.

2. Stay with Complexity

ONCE YOU'VE COMMITTED to facing a challenging idea, the next step is to stay with it, even when it feels chaotic or confusing. This is what separates people who manage to figure things out from those who give up. Complexity is uncomfortable because it's messy and uncertain. But instead of backing down, stay in that uncomfortable space. Break things down, sit with them, look at different perspectives, and don't expect clarity to come all at once. Remember, confusion is the first step to understanding. You may need some time. This is the point where most people quit, but if you stay, you'll start to notice things click.

3. Be Willing to Put in Effort and Avoid Laziness

Learning complex skills isn't easy, and it requires effort. You can't be lazy if you want to figure it out. When you first start learning something new, everything will feel difficult. It's kind of like learning to use your left hand to sign your name (or right hand if you use your left). Laziness often shows up as procrastination, excuses, or the temptation to take shortcuts. But you have to not be afraid of the work, regardless of how much you might not "feel" like doing it. Commit to spending time, consistently and deliberately, on the process. Decide you'll push through the resistance and give it your best effort.

4. Don't Fear the Time Involved

Complex learning takes time, and sometimes the sheer length of the journey scares people away. It might take weeks, months, or even years to master certain skills. But if you're worried about how much time it'll take, you'll never get started. The time will pass anyway, so what difference does it make? It will either pass with you figuring it out or with you not figuring it out. Approach it with patience and a willingness to keep going, no matter how long it takes. When you accept that it's going to take time to figure it out, it frees you from rushing or feeling pressured to "get it" right away. Because often, the figuring out part comes right after you think you'll never figure it out.

5. Surround Yourself with Resources: Books, Courses, Mentors, and Teachers

To figure anything out – you'll need resources — whether that's books, online courses, or mentors who can guide you. Surrounding yourself with the right people, books or courses can make all the difference. If I didn't have the tutorial on how to make a website, it could have taken me weeks instead of hours. This is what Elon Musk did; he surrounded himself with resources like aerospace books, experts in the field, and top engineers. He wasn't just relying on his own knowledge; he was actively pulling in information and guidance from every source available to him. Don't just rely on your own understanding — expand it by tapping into the expertise around you.

6. Trust That Your Brain Will Figure It Out Eventually

Finally, trust that your brain will figure it out eventually. This final step is crucial. At a certain point, you need to have faith in your brains ability to figure things out. Your brain is an incredibly powerful machine, capable of making connections, solving problems, and remembering details. But you need to give it time and trust the process. Learning won't always be smooth or quick, but if you keep at it, your brain will eventually put the pieces together. Trust that the understanding will come eventually.

With these steps, you're building a reliable approach to learning. It's not about being naturally gifted or knowing everything upfront. It's about persistence, the willingness to stay with complexity, and the trust that with time and effort, everything is "figureoutable." If you follow these steps, you're training yourself to become a learning machine.

So ask yourself: Where do you doubt yourself? Where does doubt show up as "lack of motivation"? Think of a goal or habit you've been putting off. Is doubt playing a role? Are there projects or goals where you feel, "I just don't have what it takes"?

Look at areas in your life where things feel stagnant or repetitive. Are there doubts that you've ignored for so long that you barely notice them anymore? Consider where you're procrastinating or avoiding decisions. Could doubt be holding you back?

Where are you avoiding complexity? Are there tasks you've labeled "too difficult" or "too time-consuming"? What would happen if you confronted them directly?

What do you believe you can't figure out? Take a moment to jot down any limiting beliefs—things you've told yourself are beyond your ability to achieve.

Are you hesitating to invest effort and time in a goal or skill because you're afraid it might be wasted?

Remember, doubt is normal. Everyone experiences it at some point. But the key is to face it head-on, identify where it's coming from, and address it.

YOU CAN FIGURE ANYTHING OUT

The main message of the chapter is this: You don't have to doubt yourself, because you can figure anything out, as long as you are willing to face complexity, and put in the effort and time. "Figuring stuff out" is one of the greatest superpowers we have as human beings.

You don't need to be "born smart" or have a special talent. You just need to apply yourself – face complexity and put in the effort and work, and you can figure anything out. If it's losing weight, building a business, passing a difficult exam or building your website – just apply yourself – and you'll figure it out.

CHAPTER 5

RELY 100% ON YOURSELF

Another hidden block that disguises itself as resistance is when people rely and hope on someone or something to come and save them.

A lot of people hold onto a secret hope that somebody or something will come into their lives and "fix" it for them. This "someone" could be a person, a politician, luck, God or life itself—it doesn't matter. It's the belief that someone or something will save you. In my experience, this belief severely limits your ability to figure things out and produce results because it puts you in a passive mindset. It reinforces the idea that you can't do it yourself, but that you need a savior to do it for you.

What I try to explain to my clients is that if you want to move from X to Y in your life, you need to use your own two hands to get there. If you're in a hole, and you want to get out of it – instead of waiting for someone to show up with a ladder – use your own hands to dig yourself out.

. . .

YOU WILL _NOT_ BE SAVED. NO ONE IS COMING.

Whatever it is—your health, your happiness, your success, your financial situation—it simply will not get better on its own.

<u>YOU have to do it.</u>

Hoping that someone will show up and show you "how" or do it for you will take away your own power to figure it out. This doesn't mean you don't seek help or guidance—it means you don't <u>rely</u> on them to do it for you. <u>You still have to do it yourself</u>: seek out the knowledge, read the books, learn, and, if needed, pay for expertise—but ultimately, **you** <u>are the one who will make it happen.</u> Whether it's building your business, making more money, losing weight or fixing your relationships, nobody is coming to save you.

And I'm speaking from experience. For years, I waited for someone to *show me* how to build my business. I made a lot of half-hearted attempts (and I say "attempts" because they weren't real efforts, more like "tries"). After a while, I started thinking, *"I did everything I could, and still nothing works. I'll just wait for someone to come and save me because I've tried everything..."*

So, I waited. And as I waited, my business got progressively worse. I was stuck. Everyone around me kept telling me to take action, but I felt like they didn't understand. *"I've tried everything. Nothing works. I can't do it,"* I thought to myself. This waiting—this reliance on someone or something else—was particularly damaging because it was making me feel more and more helpless and hopeless. And the more I waited, the worse things got.

Then one day, I picked up a book called *Can't Hurt Me* by David Goggins. At first, I didn't expect much from it, as a lot of books promise a lot but then underdeliver. But there was a section where he talked about how he was a lost, troubled kid, running from responsibility.

One day, as he was stepping out of the shower, he saw himself in the mirror and had a moment of clarity. He could see through all the B.S. he was living. The games he played with himself—feeling sorry for himself, blaming others, and playing the victim. As he stood there, soaking wet, he realized that **nobody is coming to save him**.

His dad was an abusive alcoholic. His mom was overwhelmed with her own life and couldn't help. He realized that if he was going to have a normal and successful life, he'd have to build it on his own. He made a decision right then and there to stop playing games with himself.

I don't know what it was about that story, but when I read it, something clicked inside me. Suddenly, I could see my own games—how I was also feeling sorry for myself, doubting my abilities, and waiting for someone to come and save me.

And in that moment...

I REALIZED NOBODY WAS COMING

But also, that nobody had to come. I could do it myself. I saw clearly that I had been using "I don't know how" as an excuse for my own laziness. Somehow, I convinced myself that I couldn't figure it out. I thought to myself, was I unable to read? To watch a video and follow along?

I stopped feeling sorry for myself and realized that if I wanted to succeed in my business or my life, there were things I would need to go out and **DO**. No business became successful by accident. There were pieces that made it work. All I had to do was figure out which pieces were necessary for success and then go out and **LEARN** them.

So, I went out and did that. If I needed to learn marketing, I read 10 of the best books on marketing. If I needed to learn how to sell my service, I went out and found the best mentors and books to show me how to do it. I stopped waiting for someone else to save me and went out and learned what I needed to learn to become successful. Soon, my business was flourishing.

Success in anything isn't some big mystery. It is very predictable and learnable. The big idea that I'm trying to convey here is that **you are greatly underestimating your own ability to produce results when you decide to figure it out.** You have to stop seeing the problems or situations in your life as permanent, as things that cannot be changed.

- Your unhappiness is not unchangeable. You can figure out how to be happy.

- Your inability to have a healthy relationship is not permanent. You can figure out how to have a healthy relationship.

- Your limited success in your career or business is not a "fact of life." You can figure out how business works.

- Your struggle with weight is not your "destiny." You can figure out how to lose weight.

Understand that your situation, no matter how long you've lived with it, is **CHANGEABLE** and **YOU** can change it.

If you start digging with your own two hands, you can make a difference. If you're not afraid of complexity and hard work, you can figure everything out.

So, what can you do right now? Now, right now—with your own two hands? Stop hoping for someone or something to come and save you or do it for you.

Just go do it yourself. Do what's necessary to create the life you want.

Stop hoping that someone will show up and give it to you or do it for you – and start **leaning on yourself** to make it happen. Take action towards it, and very soon you will wake up living a completely different reality.

CHAPTER 6

THE STARE-DOWN WITH FEAR

The final element often disguised as resistance is fear—specifically, the fear of failure and the fear of success.

It's similar to doubting your ability, but fear of failure is more about the "what ifs." *What if I try and it doesn't work? What if I invest all this time, effort, and money, and still fail? Then what?*

This fear often hides as procrastination, distraction, or redirecting energy to unrelated things. Instead of studying for an exam, you find yourself cleaning your room or 'doom scrolling' social media. Instead of actually starting a business, you attend seminars, read books on it, make plans—but never actually start. Instead of exercising to get in shape, you read about diets and the best exercises, never actually getting to the gym.

Fear of failure keeps you stuck in place while making you feel like you're moving. It's like running in place—lots of noise and effort, but you're not getting anywhere. You feel busy, like you're doing something meaningful, but deep down, you know you're not doing what you actually should be doing. Fear keeps you in this loop, convincing you that all this preparation, all this "getting ready," is the work. But it's not. It is avoidance disguised as work.

I have a friend who keeps talking about starting his business. He builds a website, sends it to me for feedback, and then does nothing. A few months later, he repeats the process—planning and designing but never launching. Why? He's full of fear. He's afraid of failing—afraid of being ignored, rejected, or that no one will buy from him.

What he doesn't realize is that experiencing that first failure is his first step to success. Why didn't people respond? Why didn't his offer connect? What needs to change? He could figure it out and make it work, but he avoids the discomfort of failure, rejection, or embarrassment. Instead, he stays stuck in a loop, never taking the leap.

THE WRONG VIEW OF FEAR

The problem with all of this is that we have a wrong view of fear. We think it's something to avoid, to run away from. It feels bad, so I must avoid it. But in fact, the role of fear is completely different.

Carl Jung once said, *"Where your fear is, there is your task."* The reality is that fear is our guide—a signpost showing us where to go, not a stop sign. Fear is not there to stop us—it's there to tell us what to do.

Most people are afraid of failure, not realizing that being afraid of it is like fearing the very thing that could move you closer to what you want. If you saw failure differently—as a process that actively helps you improve, rather than a statement of your worth—it could become your greatest ally.

WHEN I DECIDED to start my own business, I wasn't sure I could really do it. I had built a website but was afraid to launch it—to put it out into the world. I kept telling myself I was "getting ready," endlessly tweaking my website, convincing myself I was preparing. But deep down, I knew the truth: I was afraid of failure.

Then one evening, on my usual 10k run, I was alone, looking at the night sky, and I kept asking myself the same questions: *What are you afraid of? What is it? Why aren't you doing it?* I was angry with myself, fed up with staying stuck, and really wanted to get to the bottom of it.

And suddenly, this overwhelming feeling of inadequacy hit me. I felt so small compared to the goals I wanted to achieve. I could hear a voice inside me say, *"You? You're going to do it? Really?"* That voice tore me down, exposing the fear at its core: I wasn't good enough. Who was I even kidding? I couldn't do all that.

And that was it—that was the fear. Deep down, I was terrified that I wasn't good enough. I was afraid that if I tried and failed, it would confirm my worst belief: that I didn't have what it took. And this is why I didn't do it.

Then suddenly, it hit me—of course, I wasn't good enough! I had never done it before! That was the point! Because nobody is good enough when they start! Michael Jordan wasn't good enough at first. Neither was Kobe Bryant or Bruce Lee. They all started as "not good enough" and then got good through training and practice.

ALLOW YOURSELF TO FAIL

I realized what my problem was—I was trying to be perfect without going through the trial and errors of becoming good. I wasn't giving myself the space to try and fail and learn from my mistakes—I was trying to jump into being good enough immediately. It couldn't work!

I realized I had to give myself that space to not be good enough so I could eventually get good enough.

When I returned from that run, I immediately launched the website. I didn't care if it failed—in fact, I was even expecting it. I knew I would learn something.

Sure enough, it didn't work on the first try. I had to tweak and make changes, and eventually, through the process, it started working. People started responding, booking calls with me, and eventually, I started signing up clients.

You're Probably Not Good Enough (Yet)

Whatever you want to do, realize that you are probably not good enough—yet. But you will get good enough if you give yourself the space to try, fail, and learn. Making anything work is not a one-time event—it's a process of trying and failing until you eventually figure it out.

By giving myself space to fail and learn, I was able to move forward despite the idea that I was probably going to fail in the process. I simply became OK with it and embraced it as a necessary process of becoming "good enough."

Does Failure Mean Something About You?

In one of my favorite books, *Mindset*, Carol Dweck talks about two mindsets—a fixed and a growth mindset—and makes a distinction about how differently the two look at failure.

The way that people with a fixed mindset see failure is like a one-time event. They see it as a final destination. They believe everything has to work on the first try, and if it doesn't, that defines how they see themselves. Psychologically, it crushes them.

In contrast, people with a growth mindset see failure as part of the process on their way to becoming good. Failure is not a fixed, static event—it's part of the journey on their way to figuring it out. For a fixed mindset, it's "I don't know." For a growth mindset, it's "I don't know YET." Growth mindset people see themselves as growing into something, figuring it out, while fixed mindset people see themselves as "I should already know this, and if I don't, it means game over."

Imagine needing to pass an exam and having three attempts to do it. Fixed mindset people would have to do it on the first try. If they didn't, they'd feel stupid. If they failed the second time, they would feel even worse. By the third attempt, they would be filled with anxiety.

But growth mindset people would approach this exam differently. If they didn't pass it on the first go, they would treat it as a learning experience—*what did I learn? Why did I fail? How can I improve? What are my weak spots?* With each attempt, growth mindset people would grow smarter, stronger, and more capable of passing the exam.

This is the essence of the growth mindset: you try—you fail—you learn, and repeat the process until you succeed.

If you find yourself stuck in a fixed mindset, allow yourself room to try, fail, and grow. Failure isn't the end of the road; it's just a temporary stop. Adopt a growth mindset and see failure for what it is—a necessary step on your path forward.

Be Bold With Fear

Develop boldness with fear. Challenge it and confront it. Laugh at it. Ask it to give you its best shot. If it tells you that people will laugh at you—say you want the whole stadium to laugh. If it tells you that your business will fail—challenge that idea and try to fail on purpose.

When the founder of a particular water company was coming up with a name for his brand, he asked himself, *"What's the worst, most ridiculous name I could give a canned water company?"* Instead of running from fear, he challenged it and named it **Liquid Death**, a name you wouldn't really expect for clean spring water.

But that boldness made the name stand out in a saturated market. Today, Liquid Death is worth over $1.4 billion (2024).

Being bold with fear doesn't mean you won't fail—it means you're willing to fail, to try anyway, and to learn in the process. You are not afraid to fail.

So don't let fear spook you. Don't let it bully you. Challenge it, provoke it, and do exactly the things that it tells you not to do.

Fear of Success

Fear of success is really just another form of fearing failure—it's the fear of failing to HANDLE what comes AFTER you succeed. It's still fear of failure, just postponed.

For example, you may not enjoy having little money, but you feel like you can handle it. Or if you've been overweight your whole life, it might not be ideal, but it's familiar, and you know how to *live with it.*

Now imagine your business suddenly takes off—clients flood in, revenue skyrockets. Suddenly, you're faced with managing new taxes, hiring staff, and learning new skills. It's the sense of being unprepared for the demands of success that creates fear.

This circles back to one key question: if success requires learning something new, **do you trust your ability to figure it out**? Remember what we said in the chapter on ability – everything is figure-outable. Remind yourself that no matter what comes, you can handle it. You'll put in the effort, face complexity and figure it out.

Fear of success and fear of failure often go hand in hand, acting like hidden forces behind procrastination or not *feeling* like it.

Questions to Ask Yourself

Where are you afraid of failing? What have you delayed because you're afraid to fail—or even afraid of succeeding? Ask yourself: What am I afraid of? If I fail, what would that mean about me? And for success: If I succeed, what challenges or responsibilities would come with it? Could I handle it? Do I trust my ability to learn and adapt?

Identify how you keep yourself stuck. What would happen if you allowed yourself to fail? If you prepared yourself to experience those failures multiple times, treating them as pit stops rather than the end destination? How far could you go?

Maybe you're stuck like I was—talking about ideas, making plans, but never acting because you're afraid of failing. Maybe you want to lose weight, but you're afraid of change, so you don't start. Or you want to take on a challenge at work but doubt your ability to handle it.

Whatever it is, **decide you won't run from fear anymore**. That you won't let yourself be spooked or bullied by fear. Challenge it, provoke it, laugh at it. Run towards it and confront it. Embrace the idea of failure as a step in the journey, and stop seeing it as a testament to your worth.

Fear Isn't Going Away

Fear will always be there—it's part of the journey. Your job isn't to try to get rid of it, but to confront it, challenge it, and let it show you where you need to go. Let fear ride along, but don't let it drive. When it whispers, *But what if I fail?* respond with, *So what? I'll learn and try again.*

Elon Musk has a very interesting quote on failure. He says:

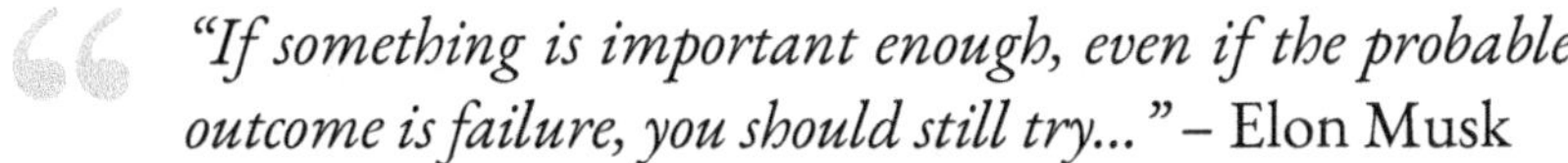

"If something is important enough, even if the probable outcome is failure, you should still try..." – Elon Musk

Honestly, it is easy to throw these kinds of quotes around and sound smart. Only you know how you feel staring at the thing you want to try, but feel paralyzed by fear. However, you have a decision to make —will you avoid it, or confront it? It is really up to you.

Yes, you might fail. But honestly, so what? At least you will know what happens. And you'll have the chance to try again. And again. And again. Until you succeed.

SUMMARY OF PART I: THE INVISIBLE FORCES

Alright, so now we've set the foundation for "doing it".

First, we talked about how you don't need motivation to do it and how motivation itself is a misnomer. You don't want to rely on motivation, rather, you want to rely on your ability to deal with resistance when it shows up.

To deal effectively with resistance, the first thing you need is **a strong decision**—a decision that this is something you truly want. Remember my story of seeing myself overweight and deciding, *I never want to be here again.* A strong decision will always outweigh weak habits, just as strong habits will always outweigh a weak decision.

The foundation of any decision is a strong reason why it matters. Reasons comes in four types:

- **External positive** (like praise or rewards),
- **External negative** (fear of criticism or humiliation),
- **Internal negative** (self-criticism and guilt), and

- **Internal positive** (doing something because it feels good to you, because it fulfills you).

For me, staying in shape wasn't about wanting praise or avoiding criticism. It was about enjoying being healthy and in shape, feeling strong, and knowing I'm where I want to be.

That's internal positive motivation, and that's where you want to root your *why*.

Once you have a clear decision and know your *why*, ask yourself: ***Could my resistance be coming from doubt in my own worth?*** Sometimes resistance shows up when we don't believe we're the type of person who does these things. Like the example of coming from a family of mechanics—it might make building a business feel out of place, like it's "not me."

You have to clear that out and decide, *This is what I want, and I'm fine with it.*

Next, we looked at doubt in our ability. Facing complexity can make us doubt we'll ever figure it out. But if you're willing to stick with it—spend 20 minutes, look at the problem, invest time and effort—you can overcome complexity. And as we talked about, effort and time aren't lost resources. They come back to you. The more you exert, the more you get back. You don't feel depleted from really learning something; you feel enriched. You don't feel exhausted after exercising; you feel stronger.

We also talked about relying 100% on ourselves. Instead of waiting or hoping for someone to come and "fix" it for you, do it for you, or save you in some way—rely primarily on yourself. Whatever you want in life, approach it with this question: What can I do to make it happen?

Then there's fear of failure. Fear of failure comes from a fixed mindset, where failure defines who you are. The growth mindset, though, sees failure as part of the process, as a learning step along the way.

Fear of success is a bit more subtle; it's the worry that you won't be able to handle the responsibilities and challenges that come with success. But if you believe you can learn new skills and adapt, then you realize success doesn't need to be intimidating.

We just went through the first part of making yourself act: recognizing what's hiding behind your resistance. The summary of it is this: If you can make a calm, clear decision with a strong *why*, let go of limiting identities, trust in your ability to figure things out, rely on yourself and stop fearing failure or success, you'll be prepared to handle resistance whenever it shows up.

Now that we have that foundation, let's move into how to deal with resistance itself.

Let's dive in.

PART TWO
KNOCKING OUT RESISTANCE

INTRODUCTION TO KNOCKING OUT RESISTANCE

Now that we've set the groundwork, and you understand all that could be holding you back, it's time to get into the real work: overcoming resistance.

Resistance is that invisible force that holds you back just when you're about to move forward. It shows up when you sit down to work, or when you plan to start that project you've been thinking about for months. It's subtle, often disguised as procrastination, doubt, or just the feeling of "I'll do it later." Resistance is powerful, and if left unchecked, it can keep you from ever getting anywhere.

The purpose of overcoming resistance isn't to fight it forever. **The goal is to do just enough repetitions to make the behavior automatic**, so resistance fades into the background.

Think about it: brushing your teeth in the morning isn't a struggle because it's a habit. You're not facing the same resistance every day, and that's exactly where you want to get with any new behavior you're building. Eventually, what you once resisted will feel as natural as anything else you do automatically.

IMAGINE A ROCKET FIRING INTO SPACE.

A little-known fact is that the rocket uses up to 80% of its fuel just to break free of Earth's gravitational pull—something scientists call *escape velocity*.

Building a new habit is a lot like that.

You're trying to escape the gravitational pull of your old habits, the part of you that wants to pull you back to what's comfortable. This is where most of your willpower is used, just like the rocket's fuel, to "escape" the pull of your own resistance.

How long does it take? Some say 30 days; others say three to six months or even a year. In my experience, **it takes about 30 days to start a habit**, but three to six months to make it a true part of you. Eventually, like brushing your teeth, it becomes something you don't need to think about.

Instead of relying on motivation, your focus is on pushing through the resistance long enough for a new habit to be born.

In this part of the book, we're going to **look at resistance head-on** —what it is, why it happens, and the practical ways to push through it.

Resistance is universal; everyone deals with it, and it doesn't go away just because you've made a decision. Even the clearest goals and strongest reasons can buckle under the weight of resistance if you don't know how to deal with it.

That is why you'll now learn **specific tools and methods to overcome resistance**, even when it's intense.

Think of this part as the roadmap for facing those internal battles. We're not aiming for the absence of resistance—because it will always show up in some form. The goal here is to understand it so well that it no longer stops you.

Let's dive into the next part and learn practical techniques to beat resistance and keep moving forward, no matter what it throws at you.

CHAPTER 7

CHANGE THE STORY

There's a story I've read in the Magic of Thinking Big, by David Schwartz, about a man walking past a construction site, watching the workers building some sort of a building.

Curious, he stops and asks the first worker, "What are you doing?" The worker glances up and replies, "I'm laying bricks."

The man continues to the next worker and asks the same question. This one replies, "I'm building a wall."

Moving on, the man asks a third worker, who says, "I'm putting together some kind of structure."

Finally, he reaches a fourth worker and asks, "What are you doing?" This worker looks up, smiles, and says, "I'm building a monument to God."

Same job. Four different responses. And each one tells you something about the person's mindset, their story, and their approach to the work.

This story about what they are doing —how they see what they're doing—determines the kind of resistance they feel, if any.

And this is where we begin the journey of overcoming resistance.

Think about it: if someone says, "Go clean your room," you'll likely feel a certain way—maybe a sense of obligation, maybe a little reluctance. But if someone says, "Let's make your room look presidential," your attitude about it changes. Now there's a different vision tied to the action, and you're more engaged, maybe even motivated.

It's the same task, but the frame you place around it makes all the difference.

This idea can be applied to any goal.

- Instead of telling yourself, "I have to study," try reframing it as "I'm becoming a doctor."
- Instead of "I have to go for a run," say, "I'm going out to build a world-class health."
- Instead of saying, "I have to work on my business", you can say, "I'm building my empire".

The task itself hasn't changed, but the story you tell yourself about it has—and so has the way resistance shows up. One story feels like an obligation; the other feels like an investment in the person you're becoming.

For example, when I was building a habit of running daily, I didn't see it as "just" going for a run. Every run meant one step closer to a new life, to a new me. With each run, I was chipping away at weakness, sculpting myself into the person I wanted to be. Just seeing it in that way made resistance feel almost non existent.

RESISTANCE IS OFTEN TIED to how we perceive what we're doing. When something feels like a chore, resistance feels heavier, more stubborn. But when the task is tied to a larger purpose or identity, resistance starts to weaken.

A simple reframe can turn a difficult task into something meaningful, even exciting. This doesn't mean resistance disappears entirely. There will still be times when studying feels tedious or when running feels like the last thing you want to do.

But by framing these actions in terms of who you're becoming—rather than what you "have to" do—you make it easier to push through.

BUILDING A PRACTICE OF REFRAMING

So, here's the challenge: start changing the story behind what you want to do. When you catch yourself saying, "I have to," stop and change it in terms of what you're doing.

Make it about the identity you're creating, the person you're becoming. Tell yourself, "I'm building a sharp, capable mind," instead of "I have to study."

Or, "I'm preparing my body to handle anything," rather than "I need to work out."

The key here isn't about adding unnecessary fluff or making things sound grander than they are. It's about seeing the task for what it really is: a step toward the person you're becoming.

This approach doesn't just get you started—it keeps you going, helping you build momentum with less resistance each time.

By framing tasks in line with your vision, resistance becomes something you handle naturally, instead of something that stops you.

You're not just going through the motions—you're actively working toward something you care about.

And that's how resistance begins to melt.

Questions to Ask Yourself

So, where in your life could you try changing the story you tell yourself about something you have to do?

What's one thing you always say you *have* to do that you could see in a new way?

What's something boring you could think of as part of a bigger goal?

Changing your story changes how you show up. When you see the thing you want to get yourself to *do it* as part of something bigger, resistance fades into the background.

One time I posted in a facebook group and complained about the resistance I feel before my runs. One older gentlemen commented, and said, *"Son, what I would give to be in your position. My knees are shot and I can not run, but there is nothing I would rather do now..."*. That comment made me realize how something I was taking as a burden is actually a blessing, something I *got* to do, not something I *had* to do.

Take a second to reflect on what are you saying to yourself before you go and do something? Do you say that you "have to" do it? Could you see it somehow differently? Maybe that you "get to" do it?

Change the story you tell yourself about what you are doing, and you will completely change how you feel about it.

CHAPTER 8

MAKE IT SMALL(ER)

Changing the story you tell yourself can help you push through resistance. But here's the truth: resistance doesn't just disappear. It might feel weaker, but it's still there, trying to stop you. And that's where a simple trick I use comes in:

Make It Smaller

When you've got something you don't feel like doing—whether it's exercise, work, or anything else—just thinking about it can often make you want to avoid it even more. And the more you think and mull about it, the harder it becomes to just do it. The key is to make the task feel small and easy, so you can't say no to it.

What is Making It Smaller?

"Making It Smaller" means breaking a task down into its smallest possible version. It's about making it so simple that it feels silly not to do it. The idea is that once you start, the rest usually follows. Think of it like starting a car with the key—something so small can start something much bigger.

Here's an example: Let's say I'm supposed to go for a 20-minute run, but it's cold outside, and I'd much rather stay inside and watch TV. When I think about running for 20 minutes, it feels like too much. So, instead of focusing on the full 20 minutes, I ask myself, *"What would be the smallest version of this activity?"*

In the case of going for a run, it could mean just jogging to the end of the street and coming right back. Or it could mean going for a 5-minute run instead of a 20-minute one. So I tell myself, *"I'll just go out for five minutes. I'll run for five minutes and then come back inside."*

Five minutes feels doable. It doesn't seem like a big deal. And most of the time, once I'm out there, I end up running for the full 20 minutes, or even longer. The real barrier was just getting started. Once I took that first step, the rest came easy.

Why It Works

This idea works because the hardest part is just getting going. Once you start, everything else tends to flow. Think about it: when you break down a task to something small, it's hard to talk yourself out of it. If I told myself, "I'll run for one minute," my mind can't argue with that. One minute? That's nothing.

Once I'm out the door and moving, it's much easier to keep going. But even if I only run for one minute, that's still progress. The goal here is to take action, no matter how small, and once you do, you'll find it easier to keep going.

I use this trick for almost everything. When I was writing this book, for example, there were many times when it was the last thing I wanted to do. But instead of procrastinating endlessly, I "tricked" myself and said, "I'll just write one sentence." That was it. But once I wrote that one sentence, I often got into the flow and kept going. If you've ever faced writer's block or been stuck on a task, you know how hard it is to start. But when you make the task small enough to handle, it becomes so much easier to begin.

HOW I DO IT

Let me share a few ways I use this trick in different parts of my life.

Working Out: Some evenings, I don't feel like going for a run. But if I tell myself, "I'll just go for five minutes," it suddenly feels like something I can handle. And most of the time, once I'm out there, I end up running much longer than I planned. The real challenge is just getting out the door. The same goes for the gym. If I don't feel like going, I tell myself, "I'll just go there for a coffee." But once I'm there, I usually end up doing my full workout. <u>The key is getting to the gym, not the workout itself.</u>

Work: I use this for big work tasks as well. Let's say I need to write a report but don't feel like starting. Instead of thinking about writing the whole thing, I tell myself, "I'll just write the draft." Once I start, the rest of the report usually falls into place. The trick is that once I get going, the task doesn't seem as overwhelming.

Reading: Reading is another area where this works. If I have a big book to read, I tell myself, "I'll just read one page." After that one page, I usually feel like reading more. It's easy to get stuck in your head and think you have to do everything at once. But by starting small, you make the task feel manageable.

Now, it's time for you to try this. Think about something you've been putting off. Maybe it's working out, studying, or a big project. How can you break it down into something small?

Here are some ideas:

- **If you have a big task at work**, what could be the minimum action you could take towards it? Could you start by writing one email or making one phone call? Or maybe even just organizing your project into steps?
- **If you don't feel like going to the gym**, could you just walk in and get a coffee? Once you're there, you'll probably end up working out.
- **If you need to study**, could you start by reading just one page or answering one question?
- **If you need to make dinner**, could you just walk to the kitchen and take out the pan? Or just chop the vegetables?

The idea is to make the action so small that it's hard to talk yourself out of it. Once you take that first step, the rest becomes easier.

THE SLIPPERY SLOPE

Sometimes, you might still feel like you don't want to keep going, even after you've made it smaller. You put on your shoes, but you still don't feel like doing the full run. You take out the pan, but you still don't feel like making the entire dinner.

That's totally normal. The trick is to remember: <u>starting</u> is the hardest part. Once you've started, you can focus on the next smallest thing to do.

Think of it like a slippery slope—you just need a nudge to start sliding downhill.

How many times have you picked up your phone to check Instagram, only to find yourself still scrolling half an hour later? You check a video, then look at the comments, then possibly reply... next thing you know, 20 minutes have passed. The same principle is at play here, except you're using it productively.

For example, instead of committing to the full run, just run to the end of the street. Once you're there, set your next goal to run to the next street sign. Or, instead of preparing the entire dinner, just start by washing the vegetables. Then chopping them.

The point is to keep breaking the task into the smallest possible steps. Each time you reach one goal, set another. At some point, that resistance <u>will</u> break, and you'll find yourself completing the entire task with relative ease.

A perfect example is my evening run. There are nights when I really don't feel like it, but I'll start by putting on my running gear. If I still don't feel like it, I'll say, "Let me just run downstairs and come back." Once I'm downstairs, I'll say, "Let me just run to the end of the street." When I get there, I'll think, "Okay, I'll just do one lap around the park." At some point, the resistance breaks, and I end up completing my full run.

The trick is to get moving. Break the task down into the next smallest possible goal and let that lead you to the next one.

THE POWER OF SMALL STEPS

Making It Smaller is a simple but powerful way to overcome resistance and get yourself to *do* it. It allows you to take that first step, no matter how small, and get moving. Once you start, everything else tends to follow.

I challenge you to try this technique in the next week. Pick one thing you've been avoiding, and find a way to make it smaller.

Write down what you did and how it felt. You'll be surprised how effective it is to break things down into small, manageable steps.

CHAPTER 9

CREATE A PRE-ROUTINE

The second trick to making action easier is something called a *pre-routine*. I first came across a similar idea in *Atomic Habits* by James Clear—a great book I would recommend if you want to understand how to create new habits.

HOW IT WORKS

Here's the idea: I run every day. And like most people, I often don't feel like it. When the time comes, excuses pile up: I imagine myself sweating, struggling, and suddenly scrolling through social media or watching TV seems a lot better. So, I created a pre-routine to make getting started easier.

WHAT'S A PRE-ROUTINE?

It's a simple action you do before your actual habit, designed to reduce the resistance to starting. For example, my pre-routine for running is straightforward: I dress for the run and lace up my shoes. That's it. Once my shoes are tied, I'm technically free to choose whether I actually want to run or just sit back down. Ironically, I never do sit down. Once I'm dressed and ready, I always go out and run. If I still feel resistance, I'll minimize the activity: "Since I'm already dressed, I'll just do a one-minute run and come back." And off I go.

Pre-routines work because they lower the "activation energy" needed to get started. *Activation energy* is a concept from chemistry, referring to the initial energy required to start a reaction. In the same way, a pre-routine lowers the energy (or effort) needed to begin a task.

Psychologically, a pre-routine taps into something called *commitment bias*. Once you've put effort into something, like lacing up your shoes or opening a book, your brain prefers consistency, making you more likely to follow through. The brain's tendency to seek consistency is why it feels natural to finish what we've started.

Think of it as knocking down the first domino - as the first one falls, the other ones follow.

Pre-routines also protect us from *decision fatigue*. The more decisions you make throughout the day, the more your willpower is drained. If starting a task feels like a big decision, the tendency will be to put it off. A pre-routine removes the decision from the equation— you're not deciding to go for a run or study for an hour; you're only deciding to lace up your shoes or set up your study area.

Another powerful factor here is the *Zeigarnik effect*, which refers to the human tendency to feel mentally burdened by unfinished tasks. Starting something, even if it's just a tiny action, relieves this mental tension. Once we begin, our mind wants to see it through. A pre-routine takes advantage of this effect by creating an entry point that's so easy, it hardly feels like starting at all.

If there's something important to you that you struggle to start, try setting up a pre-routine to make the first step easier. Here are a few examples that fit different goals and situations:

1. Going to the Gym

Set a pre-routine: pack your gym bag, put on your shoes, and step outside. Once you're out the door, the pre-routine is done. Now you can decide—go back inside, or head to the gym. Nine times out of ten, you'll keep moving toward the gym.

2. Studying

Want to study but can't get motivated? Create a pre-routine by clearing your desk, gathering your materials, and opening your textbook. Once you've done that, you can decide whether to study or take a break. Just having everything in place makes it feel natural to dive in.

3. Reading

My pre-routine for reading is simple: I pick up the book and sit in my reading chair. Once I'm there, the pre-routine is complete. Then, I tell myself I'll read just one page, but I always end up reading far more.

4. Working on a Project

If you have a big project you keep putting off, create a pre-routine that involves setting up your workspace and opening the project files.

5. Exercise at Home

Make a pre-routine that involves laying out your workout mat, filling a water bottle, or putting on exercise clothes. You don't even have to decide to start working out—just set everything up, and if you still don't feel like it, tell yourself, "I'll just do one minute of exercise."

MY STORY

When I first started running, sometimes the resistance would get the best of me, and I'd say, "I'll just do it tomorrow." Then I tried creating a pre-routine. The routine was simple—every time I wanted to go for a run, I only had to lace up my shoes. That was it. I didn't have to commit to the actual run. Once my shoes were on, I could decide what to do next.

If the resistance was still strong, I "made it smaller" by telling myself I'd just go for a short 5-minute run or a 1-minute run. That would get me out of the door, and most of the time, I'd end up doing my full run.

ADVANCED VARIATIONS

Once you're comfortable with a pre-routine, you might want to evolve it slightly. Here are a few advanced variations:

1. **Multiple Pre-Routines for Large Tasks**: For major projects, break the task into parts and create a pre-routine for each. For example, if you're writing a report, your first pre-routine might be to open the document, the next could be to jot down three bullet points, and the last could be to fill out one bullet point.

2. **Layered Pre-Routines**: If one pre-routine works, try layering it with another. For instance, if you're already comfortable putting on your gym shoes, add a quick stretch or start a motivational playlist. This helps keep the routine engaging without increasing resistance.

3. **Time-Activated Pre-Routines**: Sometimes, it's helpful to tie a pre-routine to a specific time. If you plan to exercise at 7 AM, let your pre-routine be as simple as putting on your workout clothes when the clock hits 6:55 AM. This time-based approach helps solidify the habit.

Alright, so think of something you'd like to be doing regularly but often put off or struggle to start.

It could be going to the **gym**, going for a **run**, sitting down to **study**, **working** on a project, **reading**, or even just starting your day's work at a set time.

Now, let's go through a few steps to design a pre-routine that will help you ease into this activity and make the first step feel less daunting.

Step 1: Identify Your Resistance Points

First, think about what you actually do instead when you're supposed to "do it." Do you procrastinate? Take forever to get started? Scroll endlessly through social media? Or maybe you spend time battling with yourself, debating whether to do it today or skip it altogether?

Example: Let's say I want to start my workday at 7 AM sharp. But when 7 AM rolls around, I tend to linger over my coffee or scroll on my phone. I know I should start, but I just keep putting it off.

Step 2: Choose a Small, Simple Action

Think of a small, simple action that could serve as your pre-routine. This should be an activity that brings you one step closer to your goal without requiring too much effort or decision-making. The key is that this action should feel almost too easy to avoid.

For instance, if your goal is to start working at 7 AM, your pre-routine might involve making coffee and placing it on your work desk. Or, if you want to exercise each morning, your pre-routine could be putting on your workout clothes and shoes.

Example: Since I work from home and want to start working at 7 AM, I decide that my pre-routine will be brewing my coffee, placing it on my work desk, and sitting on my chair. This simple action signals to my brain that it's time to start. Once my coffee is on my desk, the urge to start working often follows naturally.

Step 3: Test It Out

Now, try out your pre-routine. Practice it daily for a few days and see how it feels. Pay attention to whether it makes starting the main activity easier or more natural.

Example: I start practicing my coffee-on-the-desk routine every morning. After a few days, I notice that just the act of setting my coffee down at my workspace does indeed make me feel more prepared to start working. Now, instead of procrastinating the transition from morning to work, it's almost automatic.

Step 4: Adjust and Refine

Sometimes, the first pre-routine you design needs a little tweaking to fit your lifestyle better. If your initial pre-routine isn't working as expected, think about what might make it more effective or more natural for you.

Example: After a week, I find that setting my coffee on my desk works, but I also realize I need a bit more structure. So I add one more tiny step: I open my laptop as soon as I put the coffee down. This small tweak makes my pre-routine even more effective.

This exercise can be a game-changer for getting yourself to take action. By keeping the pre-routine simple, you'll make it much easier to get started on tasks.

CHAPTER 10
SHORTEN THE DEADLINE

I have a friend who's always about 10 minutes late to every meeting. It doesn't matter how important it is—he just can't seem to get there on time. One day, I asked him why he was always running behind, and he shrugged, admitting it's almost an unconscious thing—like his brain automatically resists being on time.

So, I suggested a simple trick: just imagine the meeting starts 15 minutes earlier than it actually does. "Tell yourself that's the real time," I said, "and see if you get there when you're supposed to." He tried it out, and sure enough, it worked. He's never late now. By creating an earlier "deadline" in his mind, he changed his entire approach to being on time.

This trick of shortening the deadline isn't just for showing up on time; it works for any task or project where you need that extra push. By setting an earlier date, you create urgency, giving yourself the motivation to start sooner instead of waiting until the last minute. With a shorter timeline, you're more likely to get it done with time to spare.

Parkinson's Law

This idea of setting shorter deadlines is backed by something called **Parkinson's Law**, which states, "Work expands to fill the time available for its completion." Have you ever noticed that if you have a week to finish something, it'll take a week? And if you only have a day, it'll somehow get done in that day? We naturally procrastinate when there's more time than necessary to complete something, letting tasks grow and fill that space.

By giving yourself a shorter deadline, you take control over Parkinson's Law instead of letting it control you. Imagine you have a report due in a week. If you picture it as due in three days, your brain gets into gear. You immediately create a greater sense of urgency. Suddenly, the report feels like a priority, and you're less likely to put it off.

The Final Few Minutes Phenomenon

Think about sports. Have you ever noticed how in any game, players really go for it in the last few minutes, especially when they're losing? The clock is ticking, and they play like never before, sometimes showing amazing performance. But why is that? Simple: they're facing a hard, immovable deadline. The sense of urgency makes them dig into energy reserves they might not even realize they have. They go into overdrive, unlocking focus and performance that might otherwise remain untapped.

This shows how deadlines can have a powerful effect. When you imagine the end is closer than it actually is, you stop holding back and go all in.

My Own Experience with Shortening the Deadline

I FIRST GOT this idea while pulling yet another all-nighter for an exam. Sitting there with my notes, my face in my palms, wishing I'd started sooner. I thought, *"Why didn't I start studying a week ago?"*

Sitting there, I had a bright idea. For my next exam, I decided to trick myself: I would pretend the exam was 5 days earlier than it actually was. My theory was that if I feel I have less time, I'll get going sooner. It worked. This time I also started studying a few days before an "exam", but because now it was a fake deadline, I was able to prepare much better.

When working on this book, I had a final completion date but then decided to shorten it by a month. While I didn't finish the entire book that month, I made incredible progress—probably finishing 80% of it. Without the fake deadline, I would likely have taken much longer to get to that point.

Techniques to Trigger Real Urgency

So how do you make these "fake" deadlines feel real? Here are some strategies to boost the effectiveness of shorter deadlines:

- **Put It on the Calendar**: Treat your new deadline as if it's the actual due date. Mark it with a big X on your calendar, and organize your tasks around that date. What would you do if that was the actual date?
- **Tell Someone**: Share your new deadline with someone else. Telling a friend, colleague can add a layer of accountability. You're more likely to stick to it when someone else knows.
- **Use Digital Reminders**: Set alerts on your phone or use an app. Set it so it notifies you that the "fake" deadline is near.

The key is to set realistic, slightly shorter deadlines—enough to create urgency without adding unnecessary stress. The goal is to motivate yourself, not to become discouraged. You may shorten the deadline by just a few days, say, if your school exam is on the 20th, you can set your "fake" deadline on the 15th. This way you're not pushing it, and yet you're still creating urgency.

Step-by-Step Guide: How to Try This Technique

Here's a simple guide to help you experiment with shortening deadlines:

1. **Choose a Task**: Pick a task you've been putting off. It could be anything—a report, a presentation, studying, or even cleaning.
2. **Set a Shorter Deadline**: Ask yourself, "How much time do I actually need?" Then choose a deadline that's half that time, or enough to add urgency without being impossible.
3. **Mark the Date:** Write it on your calendar, create digital reminders, or tell someone about it. Treat this as the real deadline.
4. **Track Your Progress:** As you work, notice how your urgency and focus increase. Are you getting things done faster or more efficiently? Do you procrastinate less? Do you "get to it" quicker?

NOW DO IT

Now think about something you want to do – maybe you have a weight loss deadline, or a business goal, or an exam coming up. What would happen if you moved the deadline a bit? Would you feel more charged up and willing to take more action? How much more could you do? When you shorten the deadline, you'll notice that you can get much more done in much less time.

CHAPTER 11
WORRY IN REVERSE

Think about the last time when you worried intensely, maybe right before a big exam or a presentation. How did it feel? Probably your palms started sweating, your heart rate picked up, and you could almost feel the discomfort of failing or being unprepared.

This is because, in a sense, your brain can't fully tell the difference between a real event and an imagined one. When you worry, your brain releases stress hormones and activates survival instincts to help you prepare, just in case that worry becomes reality.

The brain does this because it wants to protect you from some future event that would lead to failure, disappointment, or some sort of pain. But what if you could harness that power, using it to create urgency for the actions you want to take instead?

That's what reverse worry is about. You take your natural protection mechanism and flip it on it's head. Instead of worrying what's going to happen in the world tomorrow, you worry about what will happen if you don't do something you've committed to.

Most people worry and overthink all the time, just not about what they actually should worry. They worry about who the president will be, but they don't worry about where their lack of exercise or action will get them. When you reverse worry to do the things you *want* to do—like exercising, working, or studying—you turn worry into a tool that drives action.

How I Use Reverse Worry

When I think about skipping my runs, I can instantly start worrying where that will lead—gaining weight, feeling bad about myself, looking in the mirror and not liking what I see. I see my pants starting to feel tighter, maybe my shirt buttons pulling. That image of myself is enough to snap me out of the comfort of the couch and get moving, because I don't want that to happen.

I use it for my business, too. When I feel like putting off tasks or not giving my full effort, I imagine where my business will be if I don't get them done. Reverse worry makes me see what will happen if I don't step up now, and that quick moment of projection often helps me overcome resistance to dive back in. I'm not just seeing what's in front of me; I'm looking at the long-term effects of each choice.

Why Reverse Worry Works

Worry is deeply ingrained in our survival response. Psychologists call our ability to think ahead **mental time travel**, and research shows that vividly imagining the future activates similar parts of the brain as experiencing the event itself. Instead of using this process only for things we don't have any control over, we can reverse it to vividly imagine how we'll feel if we don't do something, and our brain will have a similar reaction, giving us that extra buzz to avoid regret.

By choosing to "worry in reverse"—to imagine what's going to happen if we don't take action and really feel that regret—you're tapping into a built-in, automatic motivator.

How to Use Reverse Worry

When you're about to skip a workout, leave a project unfinished, or give in to procrastination, use reverse worry to imagine what's going to happen if you don't do it. This isn't some long visualization process—it's a quick mental snapshot, powerful enough to feel in the moment.

1. **Imagine Tomorrow**: What will it feel like waking up tomorrow, knowing you skipped that workout? Will you feel the sting of regret or a sense of disappointment? Picture it clearly enough to feel it, as if it's already happened. When you do, do you feel instant regret? Does it make you wish you pushed through the resistance and did it?
2. **Imagine Long-Term Consequences**: For more significant habits, it can help to project even further. Imagine a week, a month, or even a year from now, facing the cumulative impact of not taking action. Maybe you picture yourself looking in the mirror, feeling frustrated by the buildup of skipped workouts or unfinished projects. Remember the image I saw in the mirror? Whenever I want to skip a workout, I think of that image and instantly snap out of it. That image works as a reminder to me how my every choice adds up over time, and I know where I'll end up.

So where can you use reverse worry in your life? Think about something you're avoiding: working out, studying, starting a project, or even making a difficult call.

To use this technique, when you start feeling like procrastinating or "I'll do it tomorrow", project yourself forward—but just briefly: Imagine yourself tomorrow, next week, or even months from now if you skip it. See the regret, disappointment, or frustration you might feel. What's going to happen if you don't do it?

Make It Real, But Keep It Quick:

This isn't a lengthy process. You only need a few seconds of clear, vivid imagining to trigger the natural worry response. Picture the outcome long enough to feel that familiar worry sensation.

Let the Motivation Take Over:

Once you see the future discomfort clearly, your brain's survival instinct does the rest, giving you the nudge to act now instead of waiting.

Reverse worry isn't about being harsh with yourself

—it's about being real with yourself. The consequences of not acting are real, and they *will* happen. So you better worry about not doing it.

By clearly seeing both the immediate and long-term impact of skipping what you need to do, you tap into your natural survival instinct to create urgency and get yourself to take action.

CHAPTER 12
FUTURE PROJECT YOURSELF

Ι f reverse worry taps into the brain's survival instinct to avoid future regret, future projection uses a different kind of pull: the excitement and energy that come from seeing yourself in future success.

Here, instead of imagining what happens if you don't act, you focus on what's going to happen if you do. This isn't about some distant, dreamy future where everything is perfect. Future projection is about briefly picturing yourself just after you've completed what you want to do to manually increase your motivation and get yourself to do it.

Here's an example from my life: When I need to go for a run but feel particularly lazy or uninspired, instead of letting resistance and inertia take over, I use future projection to picture myself just moments after I've completed a run. I can see myself standing in front of a mirror, sweaty, feeling strong and proud. I can see myself stepping into a hot shower, feeling warm water running down my back. I can completely feel it—my muscles loose, my heart rate slowing, and the satisfaction flowing over me. While worry uses negative emotions to push yourself to act, future projection is about using positive emotions to feel pulled toward doing what you want to do.

Let's say you have a work project that you're putting off. Instead of letting resistance control you, you can use future projection to make yourself feel like doing it. Imagine yourself an hour from now, having just finished it. Picture the relief of checking it off your list, feeling productive and on top of things. That positive image can make the first step feel a little easier because you're tapping into the feeling of how you'll feel once it's done, naturally pulling yourself toward doing it.

WHY DOES FUTURE PROJECTION WORK?

Just like worry, positive visualization brings the future into the present. However, instead of being based on negative emotions and the need to avoid a bad scenario, future projection focuses on positive emotions and the pull toward a good scenario. It's the classic carrot and stick—here's what will happen if you don't, and here's what you'll get if you do.

Positive future projection also creates a mental map toward the outcome, making the journey feel a little less daunting. By seeing yourself already on the other side, you're reminded that this action is possible, worth it, and within your reach.

LONG-TERM FUTURE PROJECTION: BUILDING A MOTIVATING VISION

For goals that take time, future projection can work over weeks, months or even years. This isn't about fantasizing; it's about creating a realistic picture of where you could be if you stick with it. Imagine the small wins you'll experience along the way and the ultimate outcome if you keep taking those steps forward.

If you want to get in shape or lose weight, picture yourself 90 days into consistent workouts. How will you look like if you keep at it? How about in a year? You can imagine yourself feeling stronger, maybe even looking a little younger, feeling proud every time you see the physical changes. Remember the youtuber who decided to lose weight? I can guarantee that the image of himself being able to play with his kids pushed him on days when he didn't feel like it. You can do the same.

Or if it's a business goal, imagine how your work will compound over time. Work can be time-consuming, and it's easy to forget what you're doing it all for. When I'm low on motivation, I imagine myself 10 years from now—I ask myself, how will I feel living with a super successful business? That puts me right back in my seat, ready to crush it.

Maybe you're working on a daily meditation habit, but some mornings you just don't feel like it. Right in that moment, quickly project yourself forward and imagine how you'll feel right after you do it—how centered and calm you'll feel if you take those few minutes.

Then imagine yourself a few months into consistent meditation. How will your life look? Now imagine a few years from now, when meditation becomes a strong habit. How will you feel living the life of someone who meditates every day?

Maybe you want to study regularly. Imagine yourself getting to the end of the day and knowing you've studied. How proud do you feel of yourself?

Now imagine a week of consistent studying—how do you feel knowing you've studied regularly for a full week?

Now project yourself into a distant future—when you've finished school, and maybe you're working as a programmer, an engineer, a doctor, a lawyer, a finance guy, or whatever your occupation of choice is.

How do you feel living the life you want?

Bringing It Together with Reverse Worry

Think of positive future projection as the next step after reverse worry. The two techniques work hand in hand. Where reverse worry helps you feel how *bad* you'll feel if you don't do it, future projection helps you feel how *good* you'll feel after you do it.

When you want to make yourself *do it*, combine the two techniques. First, picture the consequences of not doing it, feeling that regret or frustration.

Then flip it around and see the positive outcome waiting for you if you start. By engaging both sides—regret and reward—you create a magnetic field that pulls and pushes you towards what you want at the same time.

CHAPTER 13
THE POSITIVE POWER OF NEGATIVE VISUALIZATION

A few years ago, psychologist dr. Gabrielle Oettingen challenged the usual take on visualization in her book *Rethinking Positive Thinking*. Her research showed that focusing only on the end result we want—the typical "see it, believe it, achieve it" approach—doesn't always work. In fact, visualizing only success can often trick our brain into thinking that we have already accomplished it, and actually reduce our motivation to do it.

Instead, Oettingen discovered something surprising: when people combine visualizing the positive outcome with imagining the obstacles they'll need to overcome to reach those goals, it makes visualization much more effective.

Why? Because they knew what to expect. They could mentally brace themselves for the rough patches, the resistance, the doubt, and keep going anyway.

Think of it this way: if you want a great body, don't just picture yourself in perfect shape. You imagine the whole journey—the times you won't feel like working out, the days when the couch will feel more tempting than the treadmill, and the moments when you'll have to push through even when you're sore, tired, or simply unmotivated. Picture yourself getting to the gym anyway, putting on your workout clothes despite the resistance, doing the exercises, and then —only then—seeing the body you're building because of it.

Negative visualization is about preparing for what *really* happens along the way, not just daydreaming about the final result.

WHY NEGATIVE VISUALIZATION WORKS

Why does this work so well? It's about being ready for reality. Our brains don't like surprises, especially when it comes to discomfort or effort. So when we picture obstacles in advance, we're essentially building mental resilience. We're telling ourselves, "I know it'll be hard, and that's okay. I'll still get there."

Positive visualization has its place, of course. Seeing the reward can inspire and uplift. But to bridge the gap between thinking and doing, we need more than that. Visualizing the tough moments helps us face them when they come. Instead of stopping when resistance hits, we'll think, "Oh, this is what I expected."

Oettingen developed a strategy called **WOOP**—Wish, Outcome, Obstacle, Plan—that puts this concept into practice.

You start by identifying your goal or Wish, then think about the best Outcome. Next, you anticipate the Obstacle you're likely to face and finally create a Plan to overcome it.

WOOP works because it combines motivation with preparation, and preparation breeds resilience.

Let's say you want to get in shape. That's your **W**, the **wish**.

Next you picture your **O** – your **outcome**, which could be seeing yourself toned and fit by a specific date.

Then you imagine the **O** – the **obstacles**. The tough moments—the reluctance to leave your warm bed for an early morning run, the soreness after a hard workout, the days you'd rather skip.

Finally, you imagine the **P** – the **plan**. Picture yourself how you're overcoming these moments, pushing through, and then feel the satisfaction that comes with consistency.

Maybe you have a big project you're putting off. After you define how you would want the end outcome to look like, you imagine the frustrations: the blank screen, the moments of doubt, the urge to procrastinate.

Then you see yourself pushing past each one. Imagine the sense of completion at the end, knowing you earned it because you stuck with it.

Or maybe you need to study for an exam. Picture yourself sitting at your desk, feeling the urge to do anything *but* study.

Imagine the moments when the material seems too hard, the temptation to put it off, and then picture yourself opening the book anyway, going over your notes, and finally, walking into that classroom prepared.

By practicing negative visualization, you're not setting yourself up for disappointment. You're strengthening your resolve. Each time you face resistance and overcome it, you're building mental resilience.

And the reward? Success feels a lot more satisfying when you've anticipated the journey and all its twists and turns.

CHAPTER 14
THINK OF YOUR HATERS

ere's a powerful motivator: think about the people who would love to see you fail.

No matter how many people support us, there are always a few who would take satisfaction in watching us fail. They might be enemies, ex-friends, or simply people who don't want to see you succeed because it reminds them of their own unrealized potential. They could be anyone—a former colleague who never believed in you, an ex-partner who said you'd never amount to anything, or even family members who subtly discourage you.

Why Some People Want to See You Fail

There's a certain psychology to why some people might be secretly waiting for you to slip up. Sometimes, it has nothing to do with you personally. Instead, it's about them. Many people project their insecurities, doubts, and limiting beliefs onto others. When they see someone like you striving, working hard, and refusing to give up, it reminds them of their own goals they've abandoned, the risks they didn't take, or the hard work they never committed to. And so, rather than supporting you, they quietly hope you'll fail because your success makes them feel small. If you succeed, it means they *could have* too, but didn't.

For some, it's even deeper than that. They've convinced themselves that the world isn't fair, that only certain people get ahead, or that they're somehow excluded from success. Seeing you make it disproves all those excuses they tell themselves. You winning means they were wrong, and that's hard to face.

Turning Their Doubt into Your Motivation

When you don't feel like putting in the effort, try using your imagination to picture the faces of these people if you don't follow through. Imagine the smirk, the slight satisfaction on their faces as they think, "I knew you couldn't do it." Visualize it clearly—the quiet satisfaction of someone who is content seeing others fail because it justifies their own inaction.

Then, turn the scene around. Picture that same person watching you achieve a milestone, hearing about your promotion, or seeing you reach a goal they never thought you would. Imagine their expression shifting from smug satisfaction to disbelief, and then to the uncomfortable realization that their doubts were meaningless to you.

Make a List

If you want to take this motivation further, try making a mental list of these people. They're not on your list for revenge or anger—they're there as fuel. Each time you're tempted to skip, slack off, or give up, pull that list out in your mind. Remind yourself that while they're standing back waiting for you to fail, you're proving them wrong, day by day.

These aren't people you need to talk to or confront. They're there in the background, like quiet observers who don't believe in you. And every time you keep going, you're not just doing it for yourself. You're doing it as a silent answer to them, an unspoken reminder that they don't get to decide what you're capable of.

As an example, **David Goggins records the negative comments his critics leave online** and then plays them on repeat. Well that's just badass. Their negative words become his fire, giving him more fuel to push himself past his limits. He doesn't use his critics to seek revenge; he uses them to confirm his refusal to be defined by anyone else's limits. Their doubts don't dictate his actions; instead, they reinforce his commitment to keep going.

Think about how you could create your own version of this list. It doesn't have to be something you dwell on all the time, but on the days when motivation is low, it can be powerful to remember those doubters.

Keep Your Haters Close

Next time you feel like staying in, skipping a workout, procrastinating on your work or studies, remember your haters. Remember the people who want to see you fail and how glad they would feel if they saw you dropping the ball.

Let their satisfaction of your potential failure nudge you out of bed, into the gym, behind the books or back to work.

Focus on Your Own Growth

FINALLY, I want to leave you with this. While it's motivating to think about proving others wrong, remember that the real win here is for you. Each step you take is making you stronger, more resilient, and more focused on your own growth. Use these doubters as an initial push, but keep your sights on your own path. You're not out to prove anything to anyone—you're out to achieve your goals, build a life you're happy with.

CHAPTER 15

THINK OF PEOPLE WHO WANT (NEED) YOU TO SUCCEED

One of the strongest motivations comes from thinking about the people who believe in you, who cheer for you and who really want you to succeed. It could be your family, your partner, your mom, your friends, even people that just like you for no reason.

For me, this hits close to home. There are days when the resistance feels like a wall, and I just don't feel like doing anything. But when I think about my parents, my uncles, my extended family, and friends —all the people who genuinely want to see me succeed—I feel an instant boost. They're my strength, my motivation. When I remember that they're counting on me, it's like a light turns on, and suddenly, I can get up and do what needs to be done.

Who Wants to See You Succeed?

When you face moments of doubt or fatigue, ask yourself: *Who wants me to succeed? Who counts on me to succeed?* Maybe it's your kids, who would love to see you get healthy and lose weight. Maybe it's your partner or family who would be thrilled to see your business take off—and would benefit from your success. Whatever your goal, remember that if you don't feel like doing it for yourself, you can still do it for them.

Real Stories

Consider some of the great achievers whose lives were driven by the people around them. Michael Jordan, for example, famously talks about how important his father was in his life, fueling his desire to succeed in basketball. After his father was tragically murdered, Jordan temporarily retired from basketball but later returned, using his grief as fuel. He dedicated several victories to his father, channeling his pain into extraordinary achievements.

J.K. Rowling wrote the first Harry Potter book in coffee shops, driven by a desire to provide for her daughter. Her love for her child kept her going through financial difficulties and countless rejections, eventually leading to worldwide success.

This kind of motivation is seen in every walk of life. A single mother might find the strength to work two jobs because she's driven by her commitment to her children's future. A first-generation college student might persevere in their studies, thinking of the pride and joy their degree will bring to their parents. And countless entrepreneurs push through obstacles, determined to honor the belief that their partners or mentors have in them.

> **THE LOVE AND SUPPORT OF PEOPLE WE LOVE AND CARE ABOUT US CAN PUSH US TO ACHIEVE MORE THAN WE EVER THOUGHT POSSIBLE ON OUR OWN.**

One of the saddest stories of this working in reverse is the destiny of the footballer Adriano. He was one of the best footballers in the world, playing for clubs like Inter Milan in the Italian A League, but when his father passed away, his drive evaporated. Losing his father, he says, was something he couldn't handle. He slowly started drinking, sabotaging himself, and ended his football career shortly after. That's how powerful the influence of people we care about can be.

The Power of Supportive Figures

For me, it's not just my immediate family. It's everyone who's been there, supporting me from the start. My extended family, friends, and even mentors who see something in me that sometimes I don't see in myself. Each one of them represents a promise I've made to live up to the potential they believe I have.

Think about the people in your life. *Who would be proud of your success?* Who might be disappointed if you quit? Mentors offer guidance and help us see the path ahead. Friends keep us accountable, family shares in our achievements, and communities give us a sense of purpose and belonging. Each one adds fuel to our motivation.

Accountability: Why It Works

It's no secret that accountability makes a difference. Studies show that people are more likely to stay on track when someone else is watching. We naturally perform better when we feel that others are counting on us.

In moments of greatest resistance, remind yourself that others are invested in your success. It's not just about proving something to yourself—it's about living up to the faith others have in you. Sometimes, that extra sense of responsibility is the very thing that keeps us moving forward.

A Personal Visualization Exercise

WHEN I FEEL resistance taking over, I take a moment to visualize those who support me. I imagine my parents smiling with pride, my friends cheering me on, and my mentors nodding with approval. In those moments, it's like I can hear their voices, each one reminding me of the value of the journey.

Try this yourself. Take a deep breath and picture the people who truly want to see you succeed. Imagine them smiling, relieved, and proud. Feel their strength, their belief in you. Let that energy lift you.

Questions to Reflect Deeper

To really feel the impact, consider these questions:

- Who in your life would be proud of your success? How would your actions today impact their lives?
- Who might feel disappointed if you quit? Picture their faces, and remember that they're there to support you.
- Is there one person you could share your goal with, committing yourself to their support?

Fuel from Both Sides: The Supporters and the Doubters

In the previous chapter we talked about how to use the energy of the people who want to see you fail to get yourself to do.

But there is power in balancing both—using the energy from those who believe in you and those who would rather see you fail. When things get tough, when resistance is really strong, remember that both sides are watching. So use them both – one to go against and one to do it for.

CHAPTER 16
GRAB YOURSELF BY THE COLLAR

This approach is as raw as it gets. There are days when no amount of reasons or good intentions are enough—plain laziness is in the way. In these moments, you don't need motivation. You just need to kick yourself into gear.

This is where sheer brute force comes in. There's nothing romantic about it. You don't feel like going for a run? Drag yourself by the neck and put on your shoes. Dreading studying? Put your ass into the chair, open the book, and just get going. Sometimes, you don't negotiate; you just force yourself to do it. You pull yourself by the collar, dragging yourself where you need to be.

REAL-LIFE MOMENTS OF SHEER FORCE

I remember one time I committed to boxing every morning. It was a habit I wanted to build, but one Saturday, I woke up and just didn't feel like it. My mind flooded with excuses—"It's the weekend," "I've done enough this week," "What's one day off?" But then I got angry at myself. This wasn't about feeling ready or waiting for motivation;

it was about the commitment I'd made to myself. I literally grabbed myself by the collar, got up, and dragged myself to the boxing gym. It wasn't pretty or gentle, but it got me moving. I showed up. And sometimes, that's all that matters.

Here's another example. At one point I decided to start waking up at 6:30 a.m. every day. This wasn't natural for me, and every morning, the temptation to snooze was real. One day, when the alarm went off, I didn't feel motivated to get up; I felt the opposite. So I reached out —almost like there was another version of me with a firm grip—and dragged myself out of bed by the chest. I didn't wait for my brain to catch up. I just got up, as if a hand was pulling me forward, leaving no room for hesitation.

THE POWER OF RAW ACTION

Sometimes, there's no conversation with yourself, no time for techniques. You imagine a hand grabbing you by the scruff, hauling you to where you need to be, and you go. It's that simple. You're not negotiating with your mood or weighing options. You're doing what you've decided needs to be done. This type of action isn't about feelings; it's about being the force that pushes you forward, unrelenting and direct.

SHEER FORCE IS A SKILL YOU BUILD

Think of this as a skill. Every time you use brute force to push yourself, you strengthen the muscle of self-discipline. You train yourself to act without overthinking, to push yourself to show up even when you don't feel like it. It's a mental toughness that builds with each raw push you make, whether that's hauling yourself out of bed or dragging yourself to the gym.

So, don't wait for the stars to align or for the perfect surge of motivation. When you feel that resistance, visualize a hand grabbing you, pulling you into action, cutting off all conversation. Say to yourself, *"This is happening,"* and do it. Whether it's waking up, working out, or tackling a task, pull yourself forward without hesitation.

There's no pep talk here, no comforting advice. You simply throw yourself into the task because you've decided it's going to get done.

CHAPTER 17
BECOME THE "JUST DO IT" PERSON

Just like the Nike slogan say, "Just do it." It's simple, but there's more to it than meets the eye. Behind those three words is a world of truth about forming habits and pushing past that moment of hesitation.

The Science of Immediate Action

When a runner is gearing up for a run, they're not sitting around analyzing every reason they should or shouldn't go. There's no time for debate; it's just, "Get the shoes on. Just do it." This kind of instinctive action is rooted in the science of habit formation: the more we act without hesitating, the more automatic those actions become. Our brains create pathways to make "just doing it" easier each time.

Here's the trick: the quicker you act on a thought—within five seconds or less—the easier it is to bypass the brain's endless list of excuses. You don't give your mind a chance to talk you out of it. Studies show that this simple rule of acting quickly turns off the part of the brain responsible for overthinking.

The 5-Second Rule

Have you ever heard of the "5-second rule" by Mel Robbins? This isn't about food you dropped on the floor. It's a tool for action.

When you feel the urge to do something but start to hesitate, she says to count down from five. "5-4-3-2-1"—and just move. It's a mental hack that cuts off the overthinking part of the brain, the part that loves to come up with reasons to stall.

When you count down from 5 to 1, you break the pattern of your brain wanting to procrastinate and find excuses. So when you want to do something—whether it's making a call, starting an assignment, studying, or heading to the gym—count down from 5 to 1, and just *do* it.

Everyday "Just Do It" Moments

Think about all the little decisions in your day. You might have the thought, "I should go for a run," or, "I should start studying." Then, almost immediately, your mind begins to negotiate: *"Maybe later. I'll feel more like it tomorrow."* Here's the truth: the best thing is to not let these thoughts grow. When the thought first pops up, just go with it. Get up, put your shoes on, open the book, send the email. The moment you *"just do it"* without the back-and-forth, you're building a habit of becoming the "just do it" person.

What are you doing now? Take a moment to look at what you currently do. Are you someone who has the habit of starting things right away? Or do you have a habit of putting things off, waiting to "feel like it"? Remember, both action and inaction are habits. You can start rewriting them today by leaning into the "just do it" mindset.

It's about becoming someone who "just does it".

This isn't just about getting stuff done—it's about shaping your new *identity*. Every quick action you take will shape you into the person who "just does it". Slowly, that is who you will become.

So start simple. Make your new motto:

"THINK IT → DO IT."

Make it your new normal. Overtime, this will become the new you. People will start noticing and comment, "wow you're someone who just does things."

You have the power to re-create yourself. It really doesn't matter if you were a procrastinator in the past – you have the power to become a person who "just does it".

CHAPTER 18
DECIDE IN ADVANCE

One of the most powerful ways to stick to your goals is to make decisions ahead of time. It sounds simple, but it really works.

Here's how it goes: if you decide in the morning that you're going to go for a run after work, then you don't need to think about it again. When evening comes, you don't question it—you're going, no matter what. You've already made the decision, so there's no debate. You just do it.

Why Deciding in Advance Works

When you decide ahead of time, you avoid a whole lot of back-and-forth in your mind later. Think about it—how often have you planned to do something but ended up talking yourself out of it? Maybe you intended to hit the gym, but by the time you're done with work, you're tired, and a million excuses come up. You end up wasting energy thinking about whether you should go instead of just going, and a lot of times, you end up skipping it altogether.

But when you decide in advance, you don't give yourself that option. You don't need to "check in" with yourself to see if you still feel like it. This saves your energy because when it's time to act, you don't think—you just do.

The Science of Decision Fatigue

Social psychologist Dr. Roy F. Baumeister studied this idea and found that making decisions actually drains our mental energy. In other words, **the more choices we make, the more tired we get.**

They called this, *Decision fatigue.*

In their famous "cookie and radish" experiment, they put two groups of people. People in the first group were allowed to eat fresh-baked cookies, while others had to resist the cookies and eat radishes instead. Afterward, everyone was given a really hard puzzle to solve. The people who had to resist the cookies gave up much faster on the puzzle than those who got to eat them. Why? Because **resisting the cookies had drained their mental energy**, leaving them with less willpower for the puzzle.

When we're tired from making decisions all day, we deplete our willpower and tend to make easy choices instead of the ones we really should. That's why decision fatigue can lead us to skip a workout, reach for unhealthy snacks, or put off work.

How Deciding Ahead Counters Decision Fatigue

When you make a choice in advance, it's like you're "locking it in." You save yourself from the struggle of deciding again when you're tired. If you decide in the morning to go for a run after work, then when work is over, you don't need to ask yourself again—you just go.

You're following through on a choice you already made, so you're saving that energy.

This frees up your willpower for other things that might come up. And because you're not constantly choosing whether or not to act, you have more mental energy left over to stay consistent.

Building Momentum with Each Decision

Every time you make a choice in advance and follow through, you build momentum. This momentum isn't just about keeping up a habit; it's about removing the constant internal debates that drain your energy. When you stack these small, pre-made decisions, you're training yourself to take action without thinking. You're becoming someone who "just does it"

I started using this strategy when I committed to running every evening. At first, I'd procrastinate, debating whether I really needed to go, telling myself that maybe missing one day wouldn't hurt. But eventually, I realized that all this debating was just making it harder. So I decided in advance – *"Every evening, I am going for a run."* And when evenings came, I just went. No *"Do I really feel like it?"* The decision was already made. I saved that energy for the run itself.

How to Start Deciding in Advance

Pick one thing you want to commit to and decide exactly when you'll do it. Here's how:

1. **Set the Decision Early**. Make the choice early in the day or even the night before when you're clear-headed and less likely to change your mind. Be specific. Instead of just

saying, "I'll work out tomorrow," say, "After work, I'll change into my workout clothes and go for a 20-minute run." Lock it in.

2. **Think About Possible Excuses**. Before you reach the time to act, think of reasons why you might want to skip it later. Maybe you'll be tired, or the weather will be cold. Accept those reasons and plan around them. For example, if it's going to be cold, lay out a warm jacket by the door in the morning so you're ready to go when it's time.

3. **Don't Overthink It—Just Do It**. When the time comes, don't ask yourself if you "feel like it" or if there's something else you'd rather do. Treat it like brushing your teeth. You don't question it, you don't debate it—you just do it. Each time you follow through, it gets easier.

DECIDE NOW (TO DO IT LATER)

Deciding in advance is a simple but powerful strategy. It saves you from the mental drain of constantly deciding and leaves more energy for doing. Next time you're tempted to "see how you feel" later, don't. Make the decision now, commit to it, and act on it as if there were no other choice.

With each pre-made decision, you're training yourself to move from thinking to doing without friction. By committing in advance, you're building not only a habit but also a foundation of follow-through and consistency. Decide now, and let the action take care of itself.

SUMMARY OF PART II: KNOCKING OUT RESISTANCE

In Part II, we learned how to overcome resistance when it shows up. We talked about how resistance won't stay the same forever; eventually, it fades, and what used to take a lot of effort—like studying or working out—will start to feel as routine as brushing your teeth.

We explored how the story we tell ourselves about what we're doing, or about to do, affects how we feel about it. There's a difference between saying, *"I am studying for an exam"* and *"I am becoming a doctor."* Changing our story about what we're doing shifts how we feel about it.

We also covered some practical techniques you can use whenever resistance comes up. Since there are quite a few, **here's a quick list** you can refer to whenever you need it:

1. Change the Story. Instead of "I have to workout", say "I am building a new me". Instead of "I have to study", say, "I'm building my future". When you change the story around what you are doing, you make it much more appealing.

2. Make it smaller. Instead of imagining yourself needing to study for a full day, decide that you'll only study for 5 minutes. That's it. After that, you can decide what you want to do next. Small actions lead to larger ones, and you may end up enjoying the study, sticking with it for a couple of hours.

3. Create a pre-routine. Create a simple routine that you do before your actual task. For example, my running pre-routine is getting dressed and lacing up my shoes. After I lace up my shoes, now I am free to decide whether I really want to go for a run, or go back to my room.

4. Shorten the deadline. Work tends to expand to fill the time available for its completion. To avoid that, imagine the deadline being much shorter and often you'll make a lot more progress than you would usually.

5. Worry in reverse. Take your natural inclination to worry and flip it on it's head, worrying about what will happen if you don't do the things you said you'll do.

6. Future projecting. The opposite of worry in reverse, think about what good will happen if you do get yourself to do it. What will happen if you go and do your workout? How will you feel afterwards?

7. Positive power of negative visualization. Here we talked about how visualizing not only the finished goal, but also visualizing our struggle in overcoming resistance can significantly increase our success rate.

8. Think of people who want to see you fail. We all have people that don't want to see us succeed, and we can use their energy to give us that extra push when we're feeling lazy.

9. Think of people who want to see you succeed. Similarly, we can use the energy of people who do want us to succeed, or sometimes even need us to succeed, as a source of power and drive.

10. Use sheer force and grab yourself by the collar. Sometimes we just use sheer force to get ourselves to do it. We can quite literally pull ourselves by the collar and throw ourselves out of the house, or behind the desk, or wherever we need to be.

11. Decide in advance. Instead of wasting energy and risking *decision fatigue*, simply decide in advance when and where you're going to do it and don't waste your time negotiating with yourself later on. When the time comes, just do what you already decided you'll do.

12. Become a "Just Do It" Person. Finally, put it all together and become a just do it person. Some people are habitually late, while others are habitually on time. It's all a habit, so "just doing it" is also one. Develop a habit of just doing it. The more time you do it, the more it will become your second nature.

Now you have the tools to get yourself to *do it.* You don't need to be a victim of resistance, but know exactly how to face it and overcome it to make yourself do it.

Now you're ready for the next part, *how to not quit.* You're about to learn how to keep going and actually build a sustainable, lasting change.

PART THREE
HOW TO NOT QUIT

CHAPTER 19
THE DRAGONS AHEAD

You've reached the point where you've made the decision, you're pushing forward, and maybe you've even surprised yourself with the progress you've made. But now, we're entering a different phase of the journey—**the part where that initial excitement fades, your actions become routine, and the path can start feeling like it's stretching out forever.**

When I got a few months into running, it slowly started feeling "same-old". I would get out, run 10k, come back. And do it again tomorrow. The reason "why" I was doing it wasn't as clear anymore, because by that point I had already lost enough weight. I was getting bored with the repetitive routine of running every day, and thoughts of quitting started to form in my mind.

I felt inclined to procrastinate, to skip a day because "it doesn't matter as much". This is where my limiting identity kicked in – my "normal" of how I saw myself. Inside, I was OK with gaining a little weight because that was my old identity. Being in shape felt out of place, and slowly I was nudging myself back into my old habits.

Just to be clear, this was all happening subconsciously. I didn't consciously say to myself, *"Well OK, that's a wrap, I can go back to being my old self again…"*. No, it was all very, very subtle, showing up as a desire to "do something new" and "skipping a day won't hurt".

This is why it's so hard to create lasting change – the pull of our old "normal" is so strong, that once we get some results – get in shape, make a bit of money in our business, or do better on a few exams, the fire dwindles, and we want to quit.

Understanding the journey is crucial here. First thing to understand is that the journey itself is *dynamic*. It has its rhythm—there are highs, lows, and plateaus, and while you may think that in those moments you're not growing, you are. You just can't see it.

In this section, you will learn what is really going on behind the scenes and what to do when boredom kicks in, when you get some results and feel yourself not having the same fire as before. You will learn what to do when you start asking yourself, *"Why am I even doing this still?"*

Let's break it down into parts to see what this journey really looks like and how you can stay on track.

1. Recognize the Cycles in Progress

The journey isn't a straight line. Think of it more like waves. There are phases where you'll feel like you have all the reasons and willpower you need, followed by slower periods when progress is nearly invisible, and doubts creep in. Recognizing these cycles can prevent you from giving up when things don't seem as exciting anymore.

It's normal, and if you understand this pattern, you're more prepared to keep going through those lulls, knowing they're part of the process.

2. Realize Your "Why" Will Evolve

In the beginning, you made a decision. You probably had a clear reason for starting. **But as you move further along, that original reason will probably fade.** Over time, what motivates you may shift. I first started running daily to get myself in shape. But when I got in shape, that *why* had to change. I was no longer running to get in shape, but for something else. While I was doing my runs, I discovered benefits that I wasn't aware of before. For example, my sleep was much better. My sinuses weren't clogged. My overall mood was improved. Now these benefits became my new *why*.

Acknowledge that in your journey your why will change and evolve – and that's okay. You constantly want to redefine or even stack new reasons. Every new reason is fuel, another layer that keeps you engaged. You're not committing to an old idea of why you're doing this; you're allowing it to evolve, which keeps it alive.

3. Embrace the Boring Parts

One of the biggest truths of any worthwhile journey is that it's not always going to be thrilling. There's a rhythm to boredom, to the repetitive actions that don't give immediate satisfaction but lay down the foundation for real, sustainable progress.

During my runs, I would often look at the night sky and feel pretty bored with it. While I introduced listening to music and audiobooks, I also learned to embrace the quiet – the boring, repetitive steps became almost meditation in movement, and I've grown to enjoy it.

If you only keep going when it's exciting, you're setting yourself up to be constantly chasing the new and interesting. Learning to push through boredom without resenting it can be one of the most powerful parts of this journey. Become okay with the idea that the journey isn't always going to be enjoyable, that it will often be boring and that it's fine.

4. Accept the Reality of Resistance

There will be days where the resistance feels stronger than usual. You'll feel like everything is pulling you away from the task, and justifying why you don't need to do it will be easy.

Every time you overcome resistance in one area; you're strengthening your ability to overcome it in every other area. It's like building a muscle—the more you push against that internal friction, the stronger your "keep-going muscle" gets.

Your journey is about embracing this whole picture.

It's about doing it even when you don't feel like it, yes, but it's also about not falling into the trap of doing it while it's fresh and new, and then quitting once it becomes repetitive and boring. Instead, you need to learn to keep moving forward with a broader perspective—a perspective that sees every part of the journey, even the less glamorous parts, as essential. This is what keeps you going, what keeps you steady, and ultimately, is what makes your change to last.

In the next section, we'll dive into the practices that help you stay steady, that make it possible to keep up the momentum even when that excitement fades.

CHAPTER 20
GETTING BORED

In my journey of running, it felt like I was making huge progress in the beginning. But after a few weeks of *"doing it"* and riding that wave of momentum, I started feeling stagnant.

While the results were explosive in the beginning, after a while that fast progress slowed down and I noticed it. I felt like I was just doing the same thing every day, with not much of a reward for doing it. I started having that Deja-vu feeling each day, doing the same exercise, often running the same route at a similar time.

So I started losing "motivation". I didn't feel like it as before, and I started questioning if this was even worth it. This is a serious topic, because I've seen many people simply stop at this point. They get bored, that initial excitement of "I'm doing it!" and "I'm losing weight" or "I'm building my business!" starts waning away.

Slowly the realization that this may take a while kicks in, and the natural flow is to simply stop. To avoid this from happening, you need to understand the nature of plateaus.

How would you imagine the natural course of progress?

If you ask most people, they'll draw a line that simply flows upwards.

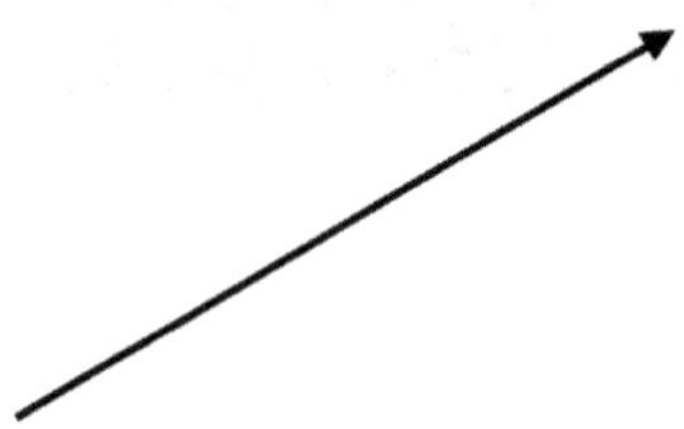

Most people imagine progress as a straight line, no ups or downs, just constant progress.

But in reality, progress actually looks more like this:

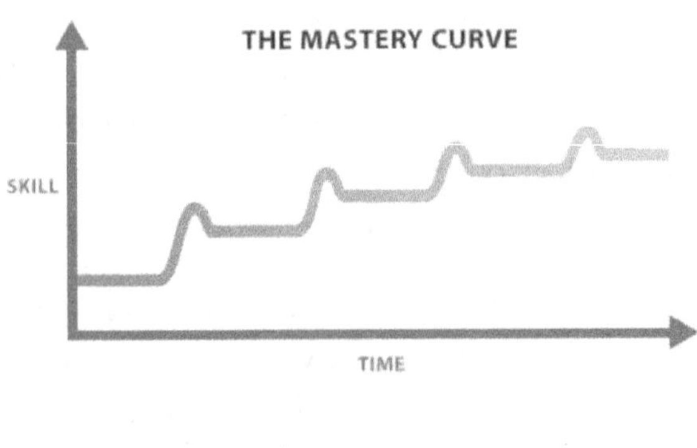

Adapted from the book "Mastery" by George Leonard.

As you can see, when you first start with something, progress begins with a sharp incline.

So if you've never exercised or studied regularly or worked on a business, it will feel like you're progressing fast. You'll feel like you're improving a lot, every day is exciting etc.

But after a while, that progress will slow down, and you'll actually start seeing a drop in your progress. Then, you'll hit a plateau. You will feel like you're just doing the same thing over and over again, without much progress to show for it.

And this is where most people stop and quit.

In his book, Mastery, George Leonard talks about 4 archetypes or types of people moving through something he calls the "mastery curve".

They are:

1. The Dabbler
2. The Obsessive
3. The Hacker
4. The Master

Let's take a closer look into each one:

1. The dabbler

This is someone who starts off enthusiastically, usually makes rapid progress, but then at the first sign of a plateau simply quits. This is the person who signs up for a gym, gets all excited about it, but soon loses interest and simply quits.

2. The Obsessive

This is someone who starts strong, gets really excited and obsess about their new thing. They really get into it, and see progress fast.

They love it! However, when they are faced with a slowing progress and a plateau, like the dabbler, they start losing interest.

They don't feel that rush of fast progress anymore, so they start doubting their own ability to really improve. Finally, they quit and move on to the next thing where they can feel the same rush again.

3. THE HACKER

The Hacker is someone who gets "good enough" at something and they are happy with that. They don't feel the need to progressively improve. For example, a hacker may pick up a few guitar lessons, learn a few songs and be completely OK with that. If they hit plateaus, they won't bother overcoming them or improving, they will simply happily stay where they are.

And finally, it's...

4. THE MASTER

This person takes their journey seriously. When they pick up a new skill or a hobby, they won't obsess over it or try to make too much progress too fast. They are in it for the long run, and they are OK with the ups and downs of progress.

When they hit plateaus, they don't stop or quit.

They keep working, keep going, until eventually they push through that plateau and reach a new level.

As an example, when I started running, I intentionally avoided obsessing over it to prevent myself from burning out. I decided to commit to it for at least 12 months, giving myself enough time to truly understand the discipline.

In her book *Grit*, Angela Duckworth explains that to build mental strength and resilience, it's important to commit to something for at least a year. She argues that within this time, you'll learn to navigate the peaks and valleys of motivation, experience real progress, and strengthen your resilience.

This is why you want to consider sticking with something for at least a year.

- **If it's a new study habit**, avoid the tendency to be obsessive—don't go all in for just two weeks and then quit.
- **If you're picking up a new sport or discipline**, a full year lets you truly get to know both yourself and the activity.
- **And if it's a new project or business**, commit for the long term to give it a real chance to show results.

THE STORY OF THE STONE CUTTER

One day, a man was walking by a stone cutter and stopped to watch him work. The stone cutter took a large hammer and, with all his strength, struck the stone on top. But nothing happened. The stone cutter swung again, and once more, nothing happened.

Curious, the man decided to wait and see how many times the stone cutter would strike the stone before it broke. He started counting... three, four, five... nothing happened. Then eleven, twelve... twenty, forty, fifty...again, nothing happened.

The stone cutter kept hitting it, yet the stone never cracked.

Sixty, seventy, eighty...

Still nothing.

Ninety, ninety-two, ninety-five, ninety-six, ninety-seven, ninety-eight, ninety-nine…

Nothing.

But sure enough, on the one-hundredth blow, the stone split in half.

Now, here's a question: Was it the hundredth blow that broke the stone, or was it the ninety-nine that came before?

This is the essence of mastery—persisting, again and again, with little to show at first, until one day, all that effort results in a major breakthrough.

THE DARKEST HOUR OF THE NIGHT

How long could you keep going without seeing significant results?

When I started my business, I worked tirelessly, day and night, for almost nine months without any major progress. People around me started getting worried and "suggested" that maybe I should consider doing something else. They argued that what I was doing just wasn't working and will probably not going to work.

But I kept going. I remember one night, after a particularly bad call with a potential client, I stepped outside and looked up at the sky, asking, *How much longer? When will I catch a break?*

I was nearly out of money, my business was struggling, and I felt lost, unsure of what else to do. My resolve was truly tested—*Did I really believe in this, or was I just saying it?*

I call this moment **the darkest hour of the night.**

When you commit to something, you will be tested.

Your mind will challenge you; people will suggest you quit or "take a break," and situations will push you to your limits. In those moments, you have to dig deep and remember your reasons for continuing.

Eventually, I found my breakthrough.

I discovered a way to position my service that made sense for both me and the market and the business took off.

So, how long would you hold on before deciding to call it quits?

In your journey, you may come to a point where you'll say: "Ahh, forget it, I just don't feel like doing this anymore."

Whether is running daily, or studying, or building a business, you WILL come to a point where progress will stall, you will get bored, and you will be tempted to switch sides or to quit.

I encourage you not to do that. Stay through that resistance, give yourself more time even if you can't see much progress anymore.

As long as you stick with it, progress <u>will</u> come. I promise you that. The stone will break and you will see a spike in your results again.

CHAPTER 21
THE POWER OF MOMENTUM

If I could, I'd make momentum the eighth wonder of the world. It's one of the few things that can truly change the game for you.

Let's take someone who dreams of becoming an entrepreneur but is scared to start their business. They doubt whether it will work, they read statistics about how most businesses fail, and they get discouraged.

But then something happens. They see an ad for a business conference coming up in their city, so they decide to attend as their first step. There, they listen to speakers, get inspired, and at coffee break get into a random conversation with someone.

They start talking about their idea, and the other person gets intrigued. They exchange numbers and agree to grab coffee sometime. A few days after the conference, our soon-to-be entrepreneur gets a text from this person, and they meet up.

After talking about the idea, they decide to create a test version and offer it to the market. They do—and make their first sale! They're officially in business.

This is a true story of a friend of mine who ended up making over a million dollars with his business.

So, what happened here?

It's the power of momentum.

The Snowball Effect

Think of momentum like a snowball rolling down a hill. At first, the snowball is small, and you need to push it to get it moving. But as it rolls down, it picks up more snow, gets bigger, and moves faster.

This is exactly what happens with our actions.

Each step builds on the last, so what once required a lot of effort becomes easier and even picks up speed. The hardest part is just getting started and making that initial push. Once the snowball is rolling, it almost powers itself. And if you keep adding to it, it only grows.

When I first decided to try running, I didn't expect it to last so long. One day, I just decided to go for a run. Then I ran the next day, too. By the third day, I felt resistance, but I pushed through and got myself on the road. By the end of the first week, I had run five times and felt great.

Sore, but great.

The decision to get myself in shape was still fresh in my mind, and those daily actions were forming momentum. A year and a half later (as I'm writing this), I completed my first half-marathon.

If you told me a year and a half ago that I'd be running half-marathons and marathons, I would've thought you were crazy. I never particularly liked running and thought a long run meant around the block.

But that's the power of momentum.

By focusing on just one day at a time and overcoming resistance TODAY, you'll naturally build momentum. It can take you places you never thought possible.

If you want to lose weight, but the goal feels too far away, remember the power of momentum.

You'd be surprised how quickly things can change.

Take the first step, let that step lead to another, and overcome resistance each day. Soon, you'll be riding the momentum wave.

Or, let's say you have a difficult exam that seems impossible. By opening the first chapter, diving into the material, and putting in effort and time, you'll soon get a handle on the subject.

Maybe you have a business problem, like getting more clients, and you think you'll never reach your goals. Start by taking the first step, even if it's small, like googling "how to get more clients as a business."

Take that small action, and soon it will snowball. In a few weeks or months, your business could be in a completely different place.

So, take that first step and let yourself catch the wave of momentum.

It just might change your life.

CHAPTER 22

CREATE A STRUCTURE YOU CAN SUSTAIN

If you want to keep up a new habit or behavior, it's not enough to just depend on your willpower to fight through resistance.

You need a structure—a setup that you can sustain for a long time.

For example, there was a time when I decided to go to the gym four times a week. I managed it for a while, but eventually, I stopped.

Want to know why?

For starters, my gym was pretty far from where I lived. I had to pack my gym bag, get to the train station, and travel for 20 minutes. Once I got there, I changed, worked out for an hour and a half, then showered, which took another 15 minutes.

Finally, I traveled back home. All in all, it was 20 minutes to get there, plus 90 minutes working out, 15 minutes showering, and another 20 minutes traveling back—2 hours and 25 minutes total.

That's a big chunk of time! After a few months, I just couldn't keep it up anymore.

The workout itself was fine—I could handle a 90-minute session, or even trim it down to an hour. But two and a half hours in total was just too much of my day. So, I naturally stopped going.

Compare that to my runs: all I have to do is get dressed at home, head downstairs, and start running. In an hour, I'm back home and showered.

It makes sense why I could stick with it, right?

To keep up a habit, you need two things:

1. PRACTICALITY
2. ENJOYMENT

For **practicality**, think about time and location.

If a new habit doesn't take too much time from your day, you're more likely to keep it up. An hour a day for health and fitness? That's a deal I'm willing to make. But two and a half hours plus travel? That's a stretch, and I'm less likely to keep that up long-term.

Then there's **enjoyment**.

To make a new habit last, you have to find something enjoyable in it.

My daily runs, for example, aren't just about exercise. They're also a time for me to be alone with my thoughts, process my day, and work through my emotions. It's therapeutic.

I usually run late in the evening, around 8 or 9 p.m., once I've finished my work for the day. Sometimes, I listen to an audiobook or some music to help me relax and connect with the moment. Running at this time helps me unwind; it's not just exercise but a way for me to let go of the day. This timing makes it feel like a natural part of my routine – a way to close out my day.

This is why I can keep up my runs—they're not just "something I have to do" but feel more like an extension of my life, a natural way to end a busy day.

That said, there are plenty of days I don't feel like running. Surprised? Even though I enjoy them, the weather, the cold, and the darkness can make staying inside feel more tempting.

Honestly, I face resistance almost every day.

And every day, I use techniques we discussed in part II to help me get going: make it smaller, follow my pre-run routine, and visualize how good I'll feel afterward.

The point is, if I hadn't found a place in my life for my runs in my routine, I probably wouldn't know how to stick with them. That's why it's important to think through where your new habit will fit into your life.

HOW WILL YOU FIT IT INTO YOUR LIFE?

If it's studying, maybe you'll do it right after you get home and take a shower, sitting down at your desk for an hour.

If it's exercise, you might, like me, want to do it at the end of the day to unwind, or maybe first thing in the morning to get ready for the day.

Find a way to fit your new habit into your life so it feels like a natural part of your day, not just something extra that you *have* to do.

To wrap up, think about these questions as you create a sustainable structure for your new habit:

- Where can you fit this habit into your day so it feels natural, like an extension of your life rather than an "add-on"?

- How can you set it up so it doesn't take more time or effort than you can realistically handle?
- What's one thing you actually enjoy about this habit that makes it worthwhile?

Remember, the key to sticking with something is making it **practical** and **enjoyable**.

By planning where and how your new habit fits into your life, you're setting yourself up for success—even when things get tough.

So, what will you do today to make sure your new habit feels like a lasting part of your life?

CHAPTER 23
GO SLOW(ER)

Most people fail not because they lack talent or resources, but because they give themselves too little time to succeed. They think in terms of 30 days, 90 days, or, at best, a year. They want results now, and when they don't see them quickly, they get impatient or start taking shortcuts that ultimately lead nowhere.

But what if, instead of trying to make things happen in months, you gave yourself years—or even a decade? When you think long-term, you eliminate the rush. You take the pressure off. And ironically, by giving yourself more time, you often succeed faster.

The 10-Year Mindset

Imagine you're starting a business. Most people fantasize about making it successful in a few months, at most a year. However, that makes them frantic, jumping steps, and taking shortcuts, which ends up taking much longer than if they took it slower.

But what if, instead of setting a goal to make your business wildly successful in six months, you plan to give yourself 10 years? Or even 20? How would your mindset change? What would you do differently if you committed to learning, adapting, and improving over a decade?

For example, when I first launched my coaching business, I wanted instant success. I rushed through decisions, made impulsive changes, and used tactics to try to force results overnight. It didn't work. I decided to let go of all that stuff and said to myself, "I'm going to be a coach for a long time. So it doesn't matter even if it takes me 10 years to make it work; I'll take my time." I focused on doing things right, building relationships with my potential clients, investing in the slow approach.

Well, it didn't take me 10 years—within less than a year, my business was growing—but only because I stopped rushing and started focusing on the long game.

When you expand your timeline, something amazing happens: the frantic energy of "I have to make this work right now" disappears, and you start focusing on doing things right, rather than just fast. And when you do that, it ends up taking you less time than if you tried to hurry through.

THE PARADOX OF TAKING THE LONG PATH

Have you ever noticed that when you try to hurry through something, it usually takes longer to get it done? That's because, in the rush, you tend to skip over important steps that don't seem critical at the moment—but then you have to go back and fix them later.

On the other hand, when you take your time and go step by step, it often ends up taking less time overall. Here's the paradox: by choosing the long path, you actually take the shorter one. When you give yourself more time, you don't rush or cut corners—you do things the right way, step by step.

When I was getting ready to run a marathon, I just wanted to get out there and run as much as I could. I thought that pushing myself harder and faster would get me there sooner. But it didn't. My progress stalled because I wasn't giving my body the recovery it needed. Once I relaxed and took it slow, gradually building up my stamina, I was ready in no time. By taking the seemingly slow path, I got there much faster.

The same thing happens when you're studying for an exam. If you skip over the basics because you just want to "get into it," it will come back to bite you later when the material gets harder. Then you'll have to go back and re-learn what you skipped. It ends up taking more time because you tried to speed things up.

If you want to lose weight, going on a strict diet might seem like the fastest way. But when you do that, you starve your body and willpower, and you'll likely quit before seeing any real results. However, if you take it slow—gradually cutting and cleaning up your diet—you'll make your results last.

Why Short Timelines Backfire

Short timelines don't just create unnecessary pressure—they cloud your judgment. When you're in a rush, you skip steps, sometimes important ones, that you'll have to fix later.

A perfect example is when I was writing this book. I made one crucial mistake—I didn't take it slow. I wanted to hurry and publish it without really clarifying my message before I started. As a result, I had to go back and rewrite entire chapters during the writing stage. This ended up taking so much more time than I had planned. If I had taken it slower and worked on clarifying the message before I started writing, it would have taken me much less time.

PLAY THE LONG GAME

To succeed, think beyond the immediate future. Here's how to start playing the long game:

1. Give Yourself More Time

Instead of aiming to lose weight in 30 days, give yourself three years. Instead of trying to grow your business by 10x in six months, aim to do it over the next decade. After all, how long do you plan to stay in shape or be in business? Maybe forever? By taking it slower, you'll likely get there much faster because you'll do things the right way.

2. Eliminate the Pressure

By giving yourself more time, you take the weight of urgency off your shoulders. This doesn't mean procrastinating—it means giving yourself the freedom and time to figure things out. When you're not burdened by the pressure to lose weight tomorrow, you can take the time to experiment and truly understand how to keep the weight off permanently.

3. Give Yourself the Room to Try, Fail & Learn

A longer timeline gives you space to make mistakes, learn from them, and improve. What if I try to lose weight and have a bad week—or even a bad month—where I gain weight? Does that mean my weight loss journey is over? Should I quit? No, because I gave myself more time. Trust me, setbacks will happen. But when you give yourself the space to experience them, you also give yourself the chance to learn how to pick yourself back up and keep going.

4. Let Go

Progress often feels slow in the beginning, but it compounds over time. Let go of thinking about the results and enjoy the journey. Don't think about arriving. Trust that the work you're putting in today will eventually get you there—because it will.

DECIDE TO TAKE THE LONG PATH

When you start thinking in years instead of weeks, you free yourself from the pressure of chasing immediate results. You make better decisions, build stronger foundations, and create something that truly lasts.

So, whether it's fitness, studying, relationships, or business, give yourself the time you need. Expand your timeline. Take the long path. Ironically, when you do, you'll often find it's actually the shortest path to success.

CHAPTER 24
FOCUS ON HABITS, NOT RESULTS

One day, after a few months of consistent exercising, as I was getting ready for my usual run, I caught my reflection in the mirror and noticed something—I was in shape. All the weight I had carried before was gone. Now, I was fit and trim. I thought – how cool is that. Then I chuckled, turned around, and headed out for my run.

I had achieved my goal without obsessing over it. I wasn't stepping on the scale every day to see how much weight I had lost. I simply focused on getting myself into my shoes, running every day, and watching what I ate. That was it.

I knew that if I just focused on doing the work every day, losing weight would naturally follow as a byproduct. Results are important —they give you direction and something to aim for. But results are not what you want to focus on, because here's the problem: results are temporary.

Yes, you might lose weight for the summer but regain it by winter. You might pass an exam but struggle to stay consistent with studying.

You might earn some quick wins in your business but fail to sustain success.

The real secret to lasting success isn't in chasing results—it's in building habits that lead to those results as a byproduct. Your habits determine your trajectory. When you focus on habits, the results take care of themselves.

The Illusion of Results

It's much easier to get some result than to keep that result. You can go on a crash diet and lose 10 kilograms in a month. That's a great result, but what happens next? If you haven't built the habits of eating well and exercising, you'll likely gain the weight back—and maybe even more.

You can pull an all-nighter for an exam and pass, but if you haven't built the habit of consistent studying, what happens when the next exam comes? And if you only study when an exam is looming, what will your study experience be like? Filled with anxiety and stress? Is that really what you want for yourself?

You might get lucky in your business and land a few clients, but if you haven't developed the habits of consistently promoting the business, attracting and acquiring new clients, your business won't be stable.

Results are just a snapshot of where you are today. Habits are what determine where you'll be tomorrow.

Focus on Habits, Not Results

I have a friend who's fairly overweight, and one day we were talking about working out. He showed me a picture of himself when he was "ripped." I have to hand it to him—he was fit. He had a six-pack and everything. When I asked him why he wasn't still doing it, he said he used to spend three hours in the gym every day.

"All I thought about was my goal of getting in shape," he told me. "But once I got there, I lost motivation and slipped into old habits."

This is the problem with chasing results—once they come, you lose motivation to continue. That's why you have to stop obsessing over results and focus instead on the consistent habits you want to build.

PATIENCE

Most people want results tomorrow. If they want a beach body, they want it tomorrow. To pass a test, they want to know everything by tomorrow. To build a business, they want to make a million dollars tomorrow. This impatience makes them focus on results and overdo the behaviors.

Let's say someone wants to lose weight. They feel motivated, so they hit the gym for three hours on the first day. They do the same the next day, but by the third day, they're burned out. By the end of the week, they quit.

But if instead, they focused on doing 30 minutes of exercise today, and then doing it again tomorrow, and the next day, and so on—by the end of the first week, they'd probably already notice some results. They'd enjoy the process instead of dreading it, which would make them stay consistent.

Look at the healthiest people in the world. They don't go on crash diets or intense workout sprints. They do small things consistently. That small morning or evening walk, that small graceful "putting down of the spoon" when they're full, that small avoidance of sugary snacks —that's what gives them consistency in their weight management.

If there's a pattern here, it's this: think small. That small walk, that small bit of exercise, that small decision to say no to extra food—it's not about starving yourself or killing yourself with exercise. Time works in your favor. Small becomes large over time.

If you spend just **30 minutes a day studying**—just reviewing the material you've covered—it might not seem like much, but over the course of a semester, it adds up to hours of preparation. Suddenly, when the exam comes, you feel ready. Compare that to cramming for 10 hours the night before—it's not even close.

If you send **just one email a day** to a potential client, that might feel insignificant. But over a year, that's 365 emails. How many do you think would say yes?

Replacing a piece of chocolate with fruit, or going for a short 10-minute walk, might seem small. But it's the start of a habit that can grow.

The Story of Three Friends

There's a story of three friends who got curious about what would happen if they committed to just one habit for ten years. They decided it would be a great experiment, so they gave it a go.

The first friend decided he would do 10 pushups a day. The second decided he would read one page of a book every day. The third decided he would eat one cupcake every day.

Sure enough, life happened, and they drifted apart. But they all kept their habits. Ten years later, they reunited, and the results were astounding.

The friend who did 10 pushups a day was athletic, in shape, and healthy. The one who read a page a day became a respected professional. And the one who ate a cupcake every day simply became overweight.

Small habits grow into big outcomes. Habits are like seeds. Each small action might not seem like much today, but over time, they grow into something extraordinary.

WHAT SMALL HABITS WILL YOU BUILD?

So what small behaviors do you need to start doing?

Ask yourself: What one thing, if done consistently over an extended amount of time, would have a significant impact on your life?

What small action could you take every day—forgetting about the results—that would lead you to where you want to go automatically? Is it going for a daily run? Cutting your meal by a quarter? Sending one email for your business?

Don't obsess over your results – obsess over your actions. Did you do it <u>today</u>? When you commit to your habits, the results will come— and they'll last.

CHAPTER 25
BUILD YOUR ENVIRONMENT

Take a look around right now. If you're at home, what do you see? If someone from the outside came in and observed your space, what would they say about you? Would they think you're organized, focused, and driven? Or would they see a place lacking in reminders of your goals, with nothing that shows how you want to live?

Every morning when I walk to my desk, I see two things waiting for me: my laptop, freshly restarted and ready to go, and a notebook with three clearly written goals for the day.

This is my way of signaling to my brain that it's time to start the day —let's get to work. You won't see any clutter, old magazines, or anything that doesn't belong.

On my wall, you'll see framed quotes that reflect who I want to be and where I want to go.

All of this is set up intentionally.

I've designed my environment—from my car to my room to my work desk—to encourage and support the behavior, beliefs and identity I want to develop.

For example, my running shoes are always by the front door, and my running gear is in an easily accessible drawer. That way, when it's time for my evening run, I don't waste time looking for everything.

In *The Power of Habit*, Charles Duhigg talks about the power of environmental cues. For example, if I want to practice my guitar every day, it's better to keep it visible and easy to reach than to store it out of sight.

Your environmental cues can either support your goals or hold you back. If you want to lose weight but keep a stack of candy on the coffee table, that's not going to help you reach your goal. That's a wrong cue. But if you replace it with a fruit bowl, you're more likely to grab an apple instead.

If you want to study more but don't have a clean, organized space, it's going to be hard to start. But if your desk is clean and organized, with relevant books on it which make it easy for you to start, now you've made your job a whole lot easier.

In *Willpower*, Roy Baumeister and John Tierney argue that willpower is limited—we only have so much of it each day. If we use it fighting off a negative environment, we'll be too drained to overcome the resistance to doing what we actually want.

Handling resistance is tough enough. So, make it as easy as possible to do the things you set out to do.

For example, if I plan to go for a run but don't know where my shoes or jogging pants are, I'm adding a layer of obstacles. Now I have less energy to fight the actual resistance of going out.

Imagine lying comfortably on the couch, then realizing you'd need to find your running clothes before even starting. It's easy to decide just to skip today.

Ask yourself: is your environment helping you do the behavior you want to build? If not, how can you set it up to do so? How can you make it easier to "slip" into the behavior you want to build?

For example, **if you want to study more**, clear off your desk and open up your notebooks. Maybe add a nice lamp to make it a cozy, inviting place to work.

Or, if your place is too distracting, consider going somewhere quieter, like the library.

(Btw, you could stack this with other techniques we discussed: set a goal to just walk to the library, create a pre-routine by packing your bag, and putting on your shoes.)

DESIGN AN ENVIRONMENT THAT SUPPORTS YOUR GOALS.

- **Place your gym bag** where you can see it, with fresh clothes, a towel, shoes, and a water bottle already packed.
- **Put your running clothes** on your bed when you get home, so they remind you to go for a run.
- **Keep your study desk clear** and inviting, and make your work area a place for quality focus.
- **Place a book** you want to read somewhere easy to grab, like the coffee table.

Make sure you design your environment that reminds you and pushes you towards what you want, instead of dragging you down.

This way you will maximize your chances of success.

CHAPTER 26
USE MILESTONES

Big goals can feel overwhelming, especially when you're focused on the end result. On low days, thinking about how long before you cross the finish line can make you feel like giving up.

This is why setting smaller milestones can give you targets you feel like you can achieve along the way. Each milestone becomes a step forward—a small win that makes the bigger journey feel more manageable.

When I used to go on long swims—often lasting over an hour—I would set smaller goals to keep myself moving forward. In the water, there were these buoys marking points every 300m. I'd set my sights on the first buoy, making it my first milestone. When I reached it, I'd aim for the next one, then the next.

Focusing on just that small stretch made the swim feel easier, and with each buoy I passed, I felt a little boost of confidence and energy.

Instead of worrying about how much farther I had to go, I just kept swimming from one buoy to the next. Each buoy was like a mini-goal, a small victory that made the longer journey feel achievable. By the time I reached the end, I'd accomplished my swim goal, one milestone at a time.

Why Milestones Matter

Milestones act as mini-goals within your bigger journey. They provide structure and allow you to see measurable progress along the way. Each milestone you reach is a reminder that you're moving forward, even if it's one small step at a time.

One of the greatest benefits of milestones is that they give you something to celebrate along the way. Hitting mini-goals makes success feel more real, which fuels your fire to keep going, especially on low days when the big goal feels too far away.

Breaking Down Big Goals with Milestones

Breaking down big goals into smaller milestones makes even the most intimidating tasks feel achievable.

Let's say you want to lose 40 pounds.

Focusing on the full 40 pounds can feel overwhelming, but starting with a milestone of losing 4 pounds feels much more achievable. This smaller goal is something you can reach relatively quickly, giving you a quick win that boosts your confidence.

Once you hit that first 4-pound milestone, you can set the next one at 8-pounds, then 20. Each milestone builds on the previous one, keeping you motivated and moving forward.

Do you know the number one reason most people cite as the reason they don't save? They don't feel like they have much to save. The idea of saving up $10.000 or even $100.000 feels so out of reach that putting $10 aside feels like a joke.

But that just isn't so.

Because if you break your goal into smaller pieces, and you say: *"I am saving up to my first $100"*, then that $10 doesn't look so small.

Once you have a $100, now you can put your next milestone at $500. Soon you'll be at $1000, and so on.

That's the power of milestones. They encourage momentum, which as we already said, builds pretty quickly.

The Journey vs. The Destination

There's a saying that the journey is more important than the destination. While the destination—the big goal—is what you're working toward, the journey is where the real growth happens.

Milestones keep you engaged with the journey, focusing on what you're doing today, this week, or this month to get closer to your goal, rather than worrying about how far away the end is.

Think of it like a long road trip.

If you only focus on reaching the final destination, the drive can feel endless. But if you set stops along the way—interesting places to visit, rest breaks—now the journey feels enjoyable, and each stop brings you closer to the finish line.

Celebrating Each Milestone

Celebrating each milestone is your way of acknowledging progress and rewarding yourself for hard work. When you hit a milestone, take a moment to appreciate what you've achieved. This could be as simple as treating yourself to something you enjoy, like a favorite meal or a day off.

Let's say you're working on improving your fitness. Every time you reach a milestone, like hitting a new personal best or achieving a target weight, celebrate it.

Go out with friends, treat yourself to new workout gear, or just take a moment to recognize how far you've come.

Celebrating milestones makes the journey more enjoyable and keeps your spirits high for the next step.

SETTING REALISTIC AND MEANINGFUL MILESTONES

Not all milestones are created equal. To keep yourself engaged, your milestones should be realistic and meaningful. Setting milestones that are too big or spaced too far apart can hurt your progress.

For example, if you set a milestone to save $5,000 in one month but know it's beyond your reach, missing it will only discourage you.

Instead, set milestones that are challenging but achievable. They should feel like progress toward your goal without being so difficult that you're constantly missing them.

DESIGNING YOUR MILESTONES

So think of a goal you want to reach or a habit you'd like to develop.

How can you get yourself moving by setting smaller, very achievable milestones?

Maybe you want to start running daily, but don't think you can do any long runs just yet.

Well, why don't you start with a very short, 5min run. Or if you can't do that, a 3 min run. Or if you're so out of shape, simply a walk around the block?

If you want to build your business, how can you chunk down your goal into smaller achievable milestones? You want to make a million, of course. But how about starting with your first dollar?

John Reese, a well-known internet marketer, once said that making that first dollar online is one of the most important things you can do. Why? Because most people talk big, but they never even sell one dollar's worth on the internet.

You want to build a beautiful body, looking like a bodybuilder? That's great, but what will the journey look like? What are the milestones along the way?

Thinking about the end result can make you quit before you even start. So don't think about the end result so much, focus only on your next milestone, and let the power of momentum carry you forward.

CHAPTER 27

GET THE RIGHT TEAM ON BOARD

What's easier? Trying to stick to a new goal with friends who cheer you on, or with people who make you feel silly for even trying? When you're working toward a goal, the people around you can make a big difference. They can be like an anchor or a sail.

The right people lift you up, remind you why you started, and challenge you to keep going—even when you don't feel like it. The wrong people drag you down, drain your energy, make you doubt yourself, or even make you quit.

For example, let's say you decide to lose weight and get in shape, and you change your diet. Well, when you tell your friends, they may not like it. They might make you feel silly for even trying.

The reality is, most people know they should change, but deep down, they don't believe they can. So, when you start pulling away, it can trigger insecurity in them, and they might subconsciously try to stop you.

Here are a few comments you might hear:

- "I don't think that much exercise is healthy."
- "Changing your diet so suddenly can put stress on your body."
- "You should relax and enjoy life a little. Life is too short."

Your support group can make or break your efforts. So, choose your friends wisely.

THE POWER OF ACCOUNTABILITY

Back in his bodybuilding days, Arnold Schwarzenegger had a buddy, Franco Columbu. If Arnold showed up at the gym looking tired or unmotivated, instead of giving him some slack, Franco would immediately challenge him on a duel. Most friends would "understand." They'd say things like, *"You worked hard. You deserve a break. It's okay to feel down sometimes. Let's go grab some pizza—you'll feel better."*

But not Franco.

He was the kind of friend who pushed Arnold to bring out his best, especially on days when he might have otherwise taken it easy.

Do you have friends like that in your life?

ACCOUNTABILITY KEEPS YOU ON TRACK

Accountability means you're not just responsible to yourself. When someone else knows your goals and is counting on you, it's harder to skip out. If you don't follow through, you're not just letting yourself down; you're letting them down, too.

Imagine setting a goal to study every night. If you keep that goal to yourself, it's easy to skip a night when you're tired.

But if you tell a friend who checks in each evening, that extra layer of commitment can push you to keep going.

Knowing they'll ask about your progress makes it more likely you'll stick to it, even on days you'd rather not.

Using Your Haters as Fuel

Not all criticism needs to be ignored. We already talked about this in the previous chapter, when we mentioned how David Goggins, uses his critics as fuel. If you have people like that in your life, consider them as part of the team. They are still on your side, only on the other side. When you use their criticism as fuel, that can give you the critical edge when you most need it.

Building Your Support Team

Creating a strong support system starts with finding people who believe in you and understand your goals. Not everyone needs to play the same role, but each person should help you stay focused and motivated.

Here are four kinds of people you might want in your corner:

1. The Encourager

The Encourager is like your personal cheerleader.

They believe in you wholeheartedly, even when you doubt yourself. This person lifts you up on tough days, reminds you of your strengths, and makes you feel capable.

For example, when I was trying to get started with recording my

YouTube videos, I had a friend who would watch every video and then call me afterward.

He would always make a big deal out of it. *"Kingggg, you did it! You're on fire!"* he'd say. His excitement gave me that small boost of confidence I needed to keep going and made every small win feel huge. That's what an Encourager does—they celebrate your progress and make every step feel like it matters.

2. THE ACCOUNTABILITY BUDDY

The Accountability Buddy is someone who's committed to checking in on your progress. They help keep you honest by asking about your goals and making sure you're following through. Just knowing they'll ask can give you that extra push to stick to your plan.

A great example of accountability is working with a life coach. A life coach isn't just there to be your friend; they're there to keep you on track.

I remember working with my first coach. During sessions, he'd ask if I'd done what I committed to the week before. If I said no, he'd seriously ask, "Why not?" and expect a real answer. I'd never had anyone keep me so accountable, and it instantly raised how seriously I took my commitments.

3. THE MENTOR

A Mentor is someone who's been down the path you're on and knows the way. They guide you with advice from their own experience, helping you avoid mistakes and stay focused.

A mentor provides grounded support and guidance because they genuinely care about your growth. I've had several mentors in my life. One of my first was much older than me—old enough to be my father.

When I made mistakes, he'd give me feedback in a calm, caring, and honest way.

Once, I missed his call and didn't call him back because I was busy. The next time we met for coffee, he gently said, "I've never, in my life, failed to return a call." He didn't need to say more. I understood, and I never missed calling him back again. A Mentor guides you with wisdom that stays with you, helping you grow from each lesson.

4. THE CHALLENGER

The Challenger is the person who pushes you to do more, even when you feel like you've done enough. They won't let you settle for "good enough," and they challenge you to break past your limits.

When I was training in Muay Thai, we had a trainer who was an absolute beast. He would push us to our limit and then beyond. I remember one of the earliest training sessions where he had us do 200 squats, 200 push-ups, 200 pull-ups, and 200 sit-ups. I thought I was going to pass out, but I finished. That's the power of a Challenger—they push you further than you thought possible, making you stronger with each step.

Your support system is a big part of your journey. Positive influences keep you grounded, motivated, and focused. Limit the negative voices, and if you can't, turn any criticism into fuel.

So, ask yourself:

- Who have you surrounded yourself with? And what effect do they have on you?
- Are they an anchor, slowing you down, or a sail, pushing you forward?

- Are there any negative voices you need to distance yourself from?
- Who could be a cheerleader, a challenger, or keep you accountable?

You might consider hiring a coach to make sure you do what you committed to. If you're in a relationship, you and your partner can keep each other accountable. You could even get a friend on board and be that person for each other.

Ask yourself, where can you find encouragement, mentorship, accountability, and challenge?

With the right people around you, it's easier to stay committed, motivated, and strong. So make sure the people around you reflect who you want to become—and distance yourself from those who don't.

CHAPTER 28
COLLECT TROPHIES ALONG THE WAY

Most people think celebrating small wins is pointless. They'll say, *"Why bother celebrating something so small? Let's be realistic—focus on the big picture."*

But here's what they don't understand: celebrating isn't just about feeling good—it's a strategy. Creating change or achieving a big goal is a marathon, not a sprint. If you're only focused on the finish line, you'll miss the joy of the journey. Worse, you'll miss one of the most powerful tools to keep yourself going: teaching your brain to crave success.

CELEBRATE ACTIONS, NOT JUST RESULTS

Here's the problem most people face: they only want to celebrate results, not the actions that lead to them. They think, *"I'll celebrate when I lose the weight, not when I go to the gym,"* or *"I'll feel proud when I hit my savings goal, not when I put a dollar into my piggy bank."*

But that approach discourages the very thing that brings results: *action.*

Progress always comes after action. No action, no progress. If you're waiting to see results before celebrating, you're missing the point. Wouldn't it make more sense to hack your brain into associating rewards with the action itself, so you feel more inclined to *doing* it?

When you celebrate an action—no matter how small—you're teaching your brain that every effort counts. Your brain is like a loyal dog—eager to please and ready to give you more of what it thinks you want. If you celebrate an action you want to repeat, your brain goes, *"Oh wow, my master likes this. Let me give them more of it!"*

This makes it easier to keep showing up, to keep repeating the actions you want repeated. Results will follow, but the secret is to celebrate the actions that get you there, so they happen again and again.

Human Nature Is (Very) Addictive

Humans are naturally wired to seek things that feel good. That's why destructive habits like smoking, gambling, or junk food are so addictive. They offer instant gratification, so we crave them.

But here's the game-changer: you can use this same mechanism to make good habits addictive.

Take running, for example. There's something called the "runner's high." It happens when you push through discomfort, and your body rewards you with endorphins that make you feel euphoric. Physically, it's incredible. Mentally, it's even better. I've personally experienced that high on many occasions. When I hit that high, the feeling is amazing. I feel like I can do anything—no mountain is too high, no problem too big, and no goal out of reach. I literally feel I can do anything.

The more I experienced this, the more running became something I didn't just *do*—it became something I *needed*. If I skip a run, I feel off, like forgetting to brush my teeth. That's the power of the brain's reward system.

Create Your Own Reward System

Some rewards, like the runner's high, happen naturally. But sometimes you have to create them yourself.

For me, this meant building a simple ritual after my runs. First, I'd take off my sweaty clothes and stand in front of the mirror for a moment. I'd look at myself with pride—especially on days when I really didn't feel like running. Then I'd step into the shower, crank up the hot water, and let it wash over me.

That shower was everything. The feeling of warm water hitting my back after running in the cold? It was incredible. My brain started craving that reward so much, it made the discomfort of running irrelevant.

And if you're thinking, *"Why not just take the shower without running?"*—I tried. It doesn't feel the same. There's something about *earning* the reward that transforms it into something powerful.

This is the secret: when you celebrate small wins, you're reinforcing behaviors that lead to success. You're training your brain to crave the actions that bring progress.

What You Celebrate Will Multiply

This principle works with any goal. For example, you may not see results from going to the gym immediately, but they will show up eventually. The key to keeping yourself going is to celebrate *each time you go.* Just the act of showing up, even on days when you didn't feel like it, is worth celebrating. That small moment of pride —knowing you got yourself there—can be a huge confidence booster.

The same applies to doing the work. The results of your effort won't be immediately visible, whether you're studying for an exam or building a business. But you can still celebrate *each day you give your all.* That sense of pride in knowing you showed up and put in the effort can be transformative.

WHAT DID YOU DO RIGHT?

I've seen this principle play out with chronic overthinkers I've worked with. Overthinkers often get stuck in a loop and are usually very critical of themselves, focusing on what they didn't do perfectly. They'd say things like, *"What I said was so stupid,"* or *"They probably think badly of me."*

But here's what I told them: Before you can tell me what you did wrong, you first have to tell me at least 7 things you did right. At first, they were reluctant, almost brushing off my suggestion as "stupid." Celebrating actions that didn't feel like "enough" felt unnatural to them.

But as they started acknowledging what they did right, I would make it a big deal out of it. I would yell, *"Wohoo! You did that right! Congratulations!"*. It almost felt stupid, but after a few times, they got into it. Soon, I would see something shifting in them. They began doing more of the *right* things, and their brain, over time, literally turned positive.

Their momentum grew, they got more confident, and the overthinking started to fade—not because they saw immediate results, but because they started rewarding themselves for things they did right.

When you focus on celebrating the action rather than waiting for results, you train your brain to crave the action itself. The more you celebrate the action, the more likely you are to keep repeating that action—and the results will follow.

Now that you've learned the importance and the effect of celebrating your actions, I want to invite you to think of your goal, your action - the thing you would like to become more consistent in. How could you create a celebration moment each time you do it?

Follow the exercise below to create your own ritual.

Exercise: Design Your Celebration Ritual

Take a moment to design a simple ritual that connects progress with a reward.

1. Choose a Trigger

What action or win will you celebrate? (e.g., finishing a workout, completing a task, or showing up for yourself.) This action doesn't have to be big, it only has to be relevant to you.

2. Pick Your Celebration

Keep it simple and personal. Maybe it's a quick dance, a favorite snack, or even shouting *"I crushed it!"* out loud.

You can get creative here. You can design your own "celebration dance", where you do something goofy like jump up and down or dance in your underwear. You can make it something cool, like standing up and doing a victory lap with your hands in the air. Or you can make it something quiet, like my hot shower after a run.

Whatever it is, make it something that will be enjoyable for you.

3. Make It Yours

The ritual doesn't have to make sense to anyone else—it just has to feel good to you. You don't have to do it publicly, you can keep it to yourself.

Write it down here:

• **Trigger**: __________________________

• **Celebration**: _____________________

Try it today. Celebrate even the tiniest thing you get right. Feel the difference it makes when you let yourself enjoy the progress.

Tie It All Together

Big wins are built on small ones. The more you celebrate, the more you reinforce the belief that you're already winning. And that belief is what keeps you moving forward.

Don't wait for the finish line to celebrate. Start now. Find one small thing you did right today—anything—and let yourself feel good about it. Dance, shout, smile, or just take a moment to reflect. Reward your brain for progress, and it'll work harder to help you succeed tomorrow.

Because, remember, *nothing succeeds like success.*

CHAPTER 29

FALL DOWN SEVEN – GET UP EIGHT

The question is not *if* you will fall; the question is *when*. And even more importantly, what will you do then?

When I was trying to build a habit of going for a daily run, I had my high days—moments when I felt like I had all the determination in the world to keep at it. But there were also days when I just couldn't make myself do it. Somehow, I found a good enough excuse, and I didn't go. Sometimes the excuse was valid—I was tired, I needed rest, or I was feeling under the weather and didn't want to risk getting sick.

But something strange happened when I skipped a day—it felt harder the next day. If I skipped two days, by the third day, it felt as if I had never run in my life. The resistance to starting again grew stronger with each passing day, and before I knew it, a single skipped run turned into a week.

This is how people fall off. It starts small—a missed session, a busy week—and suddenly it takes on a life of its own. Work gets hectic, the weather turns cold, family visits or trips happen, and before long, you've completely forgotten about your new habits.

The Mirror Moments

Remember the mirror moment I talked about earlier? That wasn't my first.

I've had those moments before. I've sworn to myself that I'd change, committed to going to the gym, eating right, and building momentum—only to find myself in the same situation months later.

And guess what? I had to get up and start again.

It would be nice to say, "I decided once, and I never struggled again," like some perfect ending to a story where I ride off into the sunset. But life doesn't work that way. No matter how strong or determined you feel, there will be moments when you slow down, maybe even fall. When that happens, you have to make the choice to get yourself back up.

Falling is Part of the Process

What does *fall down seven, get up eight* really mean? It's a Japanese proverb that reminds us that no matter how many times you fall, you simply get back up and start again.

When I work with clients, they often dive into the work with energy and determination. At first, they feel unstoppable—happy, successful, and like they've got everything figured out. But inevitably, they hit a wall.

They call me, frustrated, saying they've started struggling with the same challenges as before. They thought they've dealt with them! They've fallen. And now, they need to get back up. Most of them do.

They push forward, regain their energy and momentum—until they fall again.

This happens over and over. It's part of being human. When you're trying to make a real change—any change—you'll face this cycle. You'll feel like you're making progress, and then suddenly, you'll fall off.

And that's okay. Fall down seven, get up eight. Then do it again.

HOW TO GET BACK UP

Here's what I want you to do: prepare yourself for falling. It's not failure—it's just part of the process.

When it happens, don't tell yourself, "I can't do this. I've tried so many times, but I keep falling back. I quit." That's nonsense.

Instead, restart.

If you've fallen off working out, pack your gym bag and go to the gym—just for today. Don't think about tomorrow, next week, or how you let yourself slip. None of that matters. Just go *today*.

If you've stopped studying, open your notebook and start again. If you've been inconsistent at work, sit down and do something *today*. You fell? Great. Now get back up. Today.

People love feeling sorry for themselves when they fall. "I was making such progress, but now I've lost it all. Boohoo."

It's probably your inner child looking for sympathy. But here's the truth: your fall doesn't mean anything except that you fell. That's it. So swallow your pride, accept it, and get. back. up.

The Myth of the Streak

I ONCE HAD a 500-day streak on Duolingo learning German. I learned a lot during that time, but one day I forgot to practice, and my streak reset to zero. I was so angry that I deleted the entire app.

That's how much we value streaks. The longer we stay consistent, the harder it is to face the idea of starting over. But here's the thing: a missed day doesn't erase what you've built—it's just a stumble. The faster you accept it, the faster you can move forward.

When you start building a new habit, you start to see yourself differently. If you've picked up running regularly, you probably started seeing yourself as a runner. If you've committed to studying, now you start to see yourself as disciplined. When you fall, it feels like a blow to that new identity you tried to build.

But falling doesn't erase who you are. It's just a stumble. And the faster you get back up, the sooner you reinforce the new identity you're building.

Keep Getting Up

Here's what's important to understand: at some point, the falls will stop. The cycle <u>will</u> break. The excuses will lose their power. And the habit you've been working so hard to build will feel effortless.

Think about brushing your teeth. It's automatic now. You probably can't even remember the last time you skipped a day. The same will happen with whatever you're working on now.

You fell for the fifth time? Great. Get up and do it again. Sixth time? No problem. Get up and do it a seventh.

Eventually, you'll win. Not just over the habit, but over yourself. And that's the real victory.

CHAPTER 30
BECOME THE ONE WHO "DOES IT"

Now that you've worked through the steps, it's time to take everything you've learned and build it into your new identity.

This journey hasn't just been about finding quick fixes for motivation—it's been about becoming the kind of person who takes action, pushes through resistance, and doesn't give up when things lose their appeal.

Reflecting on the Journey So Far

Take a moment to think back on each step. From setting the groundwork, breaking through resistance, and building sustainable habits, you now have the tools to make real progress.

This isn't just a list of techniques—it's a mindset shift.

Commit to Consistency

The real key to lasting change is consistency. Motivation may come and go, but following through is what brings results.

Make a commitment to continue setting small goals, celebrating each win, and refining your environment to support your efforts.

Embrace the Challenges

Along the way, there will be setbacks and plateaus. Use what you've learned about overcoming resistance and maintaining momentum to handle these challenges.

Remind yourself that every successful person faces obstacles—what sets them apart is their ability to push through.

Final Thoughts

As you move forward, remember that your journey is about steady growth.

The ultimate goal is not just to reach a specific milestone but to become the kind of person who is resilient, committed, and unshakable in the pursuit of their goals.

Ask Yourself:

- How will you keep building momentum?
- What small wins can you continue to celebrate?
- Who can you rely on for support?

Becoming the person who follows through is a journey, but you've already taken the first steps.

Keep going, keep growing, and remember that you're capable of achieving anything you set your mind to.

BEYOND MOTIVATION – NOW IT'S UP TO YOU

You've made it to the end of the book, but if there's one thing I want to emphasize here, it's this: reaching the end isn't where the change happens. It happens when you take these ideas and start putting them to work in your life.

This isn't a journey where motivation will now suddenly kick in and everything will flow easily. *Motivation isn't what got you here.* What's gotten you here is **action**: the decision to open this book, to read through it, and the willingness to keep reading even in moments when you didn't "feel like it" anymore.

The message of this book is clear - you don't have to wait until you *feel* like it to do it. The people who get things done, who build habits, accomplish goals, and make things happen, aren't people who *feel* like it every day. They're people who *do it* anyway.

Whether it's by creating a pre-routine to get you moving, using sheer force to push yourself, or reminding yourself of the people who believe in you, you have more options than just "waiting until the right moment." You're now armed with practical tools that let you bypass the struggle with resistance and get yourself to doing.

As you move forward, **redefine what success and failure mean to you.** Success doesn't have to look like a constant upward climb. Some days, success will be showing up at all, even if it's messy. Failure isn't something to fear; it's a part of the process. It's proof that you're moving forward, making mistakes, learning, and adapting. Expect it. Embrace it. Move through it.

There will be times when you fall off track, when things get tough, when the thought of continuing feels exhausting and when the thought of quitting almost sounds reasonable. It's okay. This is part of the journey. Your resilience will get stronger each time you pick yourself up and push forward, even after a setback.

If you take away one piece of advice from this book, it's this: **start now.** You don't need the perfect plan, nor do you need to feel completely prepared. Pick <u>one</u> area—whether it's your health, your career, or even a small personal goal you've been putting off—and choose <u>one</u> action to start with. Make it so small that you know you can do it. Then, do it again tomorrow.

Small actions compound. The momentum you build from starting today, however small, will make it easier to keep going. Let this be the starting point. Give yourself permission to start wherever you are, with whatever you have.

Becoming the Person Who Does It

Ultimately, this book is here to help you become a person who *does it*, even if – and *especially* when – you don't feel like it. A person who doesn't wait around, doesn't get caught in endless debates with themselves, and doesn't rely on the fleeting feeling of motivation to get going. You've learned the skills to become that person. Now it's time to use them.

The choice is yours, every day, to do or not to do. To make things happen or to put them off. To be someone who does or someone who waits. The power is in your hands. Go out there, and make it happen.

MY CHALLENGE TO YOU

Now you've reached the end of this book. You've covered a lot, and by now, you should have a strong sense that you can get yourself to do it—whatever "it" may be.

Whenever I finish a book, I like to skim through it, then close it, and reflect. I ask myself: *What was the author trying to tell me? What did I take away from this book?*

This quick exercise helps me clarify the key insights I've gained.

But I don't want you to just stay with insights and impressions. I want you to actually *do* something with them. The real gift of this book is if it inspires you to start doing something you've always wanted to do but struggled to stay consistent with.

It could be exercising, studying, working on your business, meditating, preparing healthy meals, reading, or simply spending quiet time with yourself. Something that requires discipline.

You'll gain the most from this book if you choose **one thing** and experiment with it.

So here's my challenge for you:

Take that **one thing** and commit to it for the next <u>12 months</u>. Not one month, not three months—twelve.

Why? Because a 12-month commitment gives you the chance to go on a journey of self-discovery. How long will you stick with it before you get bored, distracted, or tempted by a shiny new object? Can you challenge yourself to stay committed to it for an entire year?

Bruce Lee once said, *"All knowledge ultimately leads to self-knowledge."* That's why I want you to commit to 12 months—so you can learn about yourself. You'll see the games you play with yourself, the ways you trick yourself, how you escape discomfort, and how you quit when things get tough.

You may have quit on everything so far. But maybe this time, you don't quit on this **one thing.**

For me, it was running. I'll be honest—I didn't commit to running every single day. I wanted rest days, and I knew running every day wouldn't be realistic for me. Life happens. My goal was to create a habit I could sustain forever.

Over those 12 months, there were stretches where I stayed consistent for weeks on end. But there were also times when I dropped off completely—I'd go an entire week without running. The difference was, because I had committed to 12 months, I always came back.

The problem isn't falling off—that's normal. The challenge is getting back on track.

Let me share a story about one of my clients—let's call him Rudy. When we started working together, Rudy was excited about committing to his **one thing.** He decided he'd go to the gym every day.

At first, he was consistent—sending me pictures from the gym, motivational videos, updates about his workouts. He was on top of it.

Then I suddenly stopped hearing from him. When I reached out, he said he'd "fallen off" and that life had been "weird." As if that had anything to do with him getting to the gym.

Rudy eventually picked himself back up and started going again. He sent more pictures, more updates, and once again, he was all in.

And then, it happened again. I stopped hearing from him.

This cycle repeated a few times.

What Rudy learned—and what you'll learn—is that when you commit to 12 months, you get to know yourself deeply. You'll recognize your patterns, the highs and lows, the ways you hold yourself back. And, most importantly, you'll train yourself to push through.

If you've developed a habit of falling off from things, committing to 12 months will change your life.

And here's something I've come to realize through this process: self-discipline is actually the ultimate expression of self-love. When you go and do that **one thing** that is important to you, even when you don't feel like it, that is when you show that you actually care about yourself.

So, do you accept my challenge? Are you willing to pick **one thing** and stick with it for at least 12 months?

If yes, please write your commitment on the next page:

I, [Your Name], hereby commit, to doing [your one thing] for the next 12 months and not quit, no matter what.

____

____

____

____

Remember, if you fall off, that's okay—just get back to it. No matter how much you think you've "ruined" your progress, simply pick it back up from where you left off.

I wish you the best of luck, and I hope to see you in the Screw Motivation community or one of my programs in the future.

To your success,

Omir Dzelilovic

ABOUT THE AUTHOR

Omir Dzelilovic is a renowned personal development coach with over a decade of experience helping individuals unlock their full potential. Having worked with hundreds of clients from across the globe, he specializes in guiding people through challenges and empowering them to overcome self-doubt, procrastination, and fear of failure. He is the author of Afraid to Fail?, which achieved the #1 spot on Amazon's bestseller list. His transformative approach to personal growth combines actionable strategies with deep insight, making his work accessible and impactful for readers and clients alike. When he's not coaching or writing, Omir is dedicated to ongoing learning and connecting with individuals passionate about self-improvement and personal transformation. You can find more about him at www.coachomir.com

 instagram.com/coachomir

linkedin.com/in/omir-dzelilovic

RECOMMENDED READING

These books offer additional insights and techniques that complement the strategies in *Screw Motivation: Why You Don't Have to Feel Like It to Do It.* Whether you're looking to deepen your understanding of habit formation, strengthen your resilience, or explore new ways to cultivate a powerful mindset, these resources can support you on your journey.

1. Mindset: The New Psychology of Success by *Carol S. Dweck*
2. Can't Hurt Me: Master Your Mind and Defy the Odds by *David Goggins*
3. Never Finished: Unshackle Your Mind and Win the War Within *by David Goggins*
4. Atomic Habits: An Easy & Proven Way to Build Good Habits & Break Bad Ones by *James Clear*
5. The Power of Habit: Why We Do What We Do in Life and Business by *Charles Duhigg*
6. Deep Work: Rules for Focused Success in a Distracted World by *Cal Newport*
7. Finish: Give Yourself the Gift of Done by *Jon Acuff*
8. The War of Art: Break Through the Blocks and Win Your Inner Creative Battles by *Steven Pressfield*
9. Grit: The Power of Passion and Perseverance by *Angela Duckworth*
10. Drive: The Surprising Truth About What Motivates Us by *Daniel H. Pink*
11. Tiny Habits: The Small Changes That Change Everything by *BJ Fogg*

www.ingramcontent.com/pod-product-compliance
Lightning Source LLC
LaVergne TN
LVHW010513200726
843506LV00013B/2584